THE RADICAL SUBURB

THE
RADICAL SUBURB

SOUNDINGS IN CHANGING
AMERICAN CHARACTER

by
John B. Orr
and
F. Patrick Nichelson

THE WESTMINSTER PRESS
Philadelphia

ISBN 0–664–24881–0

LIBRARY OF CONGRESS CATALOG CARD NO. 78–110084

Published by The Westminster Press®
Philadelphia, Pennsylvania

PRINTED IN THE UNITED STATES OF AMERICA

CONTENTS

PREFACE

THE FOLLOWING CHAPTERS represent a minor exercise in the ethics of listening. People normally think of ethics as anything but a listening process. According to the usual understanding, ethicists are preachers. We hire ethicists to tell us what to do, and then to bless our doing it. The model in this view is that of a blueprint maker, one who maps out ahead of time the oughtness of situations and deeds.

Many college-educated people are reminded of the public cartoon of a man like Bertrand Russell when they hear the word "ethics." The ethicist is a domineering utopia builder, fulminating against structures that do not match up. Or they think of the stereotypical Reinhold Niebuhr, writing volumes in his effort to reflect on the height and depth of power politics, and therefore in his effort to be an effective political presence. Such images mislead us not only from understanding the ethical work of a Russell or a Niebuhr but more so from grasping the nature of ethics as the discipline is mainly carried on. Most work in ethics, whether it is rationalist or emotivist, philosophical or religious, is founded on listening. By profession, the ethicist does modest work. He listens to the stories people tell about themselves—the ways they speak about what it means to be fully human.

This book is the result of listening to contemporary middle-class suburbanites tell their stories. The listening has been enjoyable but difficult. It is not easy to listen to one's own cultural story with aural discrimination and acuity. Our ears are attracted by the novel, not by the conventional sounds always around us. So it is no surprise that our interests in ethics, as in anthropology, are often directed toward the alien, the bizarre, and even the practically irrelevant. To listen to family stories, the stories that have shaped us and continue to do so, requires a certain patience. But, in approaching middle-class morality, the fruits of patient listening can be surprising. To be honest, we must admit our amazement with a new turn in the suburban family tale; we expected the redundant and the cliché, and instead discovered the fascinating. What we had written off as standard static came through with a different but clear signal.

No doubt one can guess from the title of this book that something different from the traditional antiseptic suburban story has been heard. One can guess, also, that there are wild stories floating about in middle-class havens, and that they will be reported here. It is the intent of this book to fill in some of the content of these stories. But first, some introductory words are in order, because a special kind of listening and reporting has been utilized.

In the first place, the listening component of the ethical enterprise has been quite self-consciously emphasized. While all ethics are founded on listening, the bias here is that the listening should continue to the end of a project, as it does, for example, in nondirective psychotherapy. That is, the authors have wanted to correct what they regard as an omission in many ethical studies. Ethics, at least by the time they are formulated in textbooks and essays, are often separated from what might be called moral history, and they can easily assume a strange spirit of abstraction. If the ethicist is uninterested in reporting his data, we feel that he has stripped his work of its flesh and, perhaps out of modesty, has too narrowly defined the scope of his discipline.

So this is not a book on the sociology of the suburb; nor is it in any sense meant as a comprehensive history of American suburbs. It is a book about suburban ethics within the context of American character. It is an exploration into the moral history of the modern middle class, and it is also a suggestion as to the ethical logic of that moral history.

Readers will quickly detect that the listening and reporting are of a special kind because of the use of ideal types. There will be talk about expansive man and conscientious man, savage styles and radical styles. That is, ideal types will be projected both to aid listening and to make reporting manageable. The types will be used forthrightly and pointedly. Why? Because that is the way the human mind works, and that is the way we hear things. To talk about expansive man is no more nor less blithe than talking about womanly personality, Japanese character, capitalist feelings, Christian attitudes, or adolescence. We use ideal types because they explain our experience. But the types inevitably shape our experience too, just as a cosmic myth both explains nature and fashions one's next encounter with nature.

The ideal types in this book will largely have to do with suburban mentalities. The types will say something about suburbanites and their ways of imagining themselves and their surroundings. Making the types so blatant will encourage a certain wakeful listening. There are savages out there. Have you seen any? There is an emerging cadre of affluent persons who are redefining what "radical" means. Don't you agree? To answer questions, we create generalizations; we are trying to domesticate the chaotic flow of experiences into something manageable. Anyone who thinks he can avoid this generalizing process is naïve. The thing to do is to be conscious of the process.

Of course, ideal types are not like the hole in a dough-
nut, merely nothing, or a simple creation of one's subjective
imagination. When we speak about the radical, expansive
man, we are speaking about real people and real tendencies.
The typology has evolved, in other words, from listening,
from case studies, and from testing reactions of people. The
ethicist, like the therapist, listens, imagines, and then, symbolically, he recounts the story to the storyteller. If the symbolic account rings true, if the reader finds himself in it,
then the ethicist knows he has accomplished something important. The symbolic account rendered here has already
been tested, and at least a few suburbanites, sometimes
gleefully and sometimes in fury, have given the nod. They
have discovered themselves here, and what they have found
is that the suburban family story has a new plot.

What happened was that a listening game was played,
and while only the authors can take responsibility for the
final account, the following instructors and students at the
University of Southern California had a special part in the
fun: Gracia Fay and Robert Ellwood, Wilbur J. Bennett,
Pat Armstrong, Jane Bloomfield, Riv-Ellen Prell, and Ste-
ven Foldes.

As will be clear to many, Ernst Cassirer, the philosopher, and H. Richard Niebuhr, the theologian, are for the
authors pioneers in the ethics of listening. In a less playful
book, more careful and devoted attention would have been
paid to these two. Here we might just mention for the den,
or poolside, Cassirer's *An Essay on Man* and Niebuhr's
The Responsible Self.

A central conclusion of our study is that "playful" is not
a bad word. However heterodox this discovery of the radical suburb may sound to our sober hearing, it has profound roots in our past. Neither in the Bible nor in classical
antiquity was man viewed as created to work. The recent
notion of man-the-worker, so beautifully exposed by Josef

Pieper's book *Leisure: The Basis of Culture* is the true heresy. Man was made to play. However much in different periods and places he may be tied to servile necessities and repressive social duties, there is something in man that soars beyond work. As Aquinas phrased it, man's highest ordination is to the life of contemplation, and contemplation is high-level, delicious play.

When the radical suburbanite affirms the importance of play in all its forms—spiritual and physical—he is doing something very "serious." He is making a worthwhile contribution to the prevailing moral ethos. Play is serious, he is saying. Play sums up what it means to be human, and it has a kind of normativeness to it. There is a playful rule book, and in the suburbs this rule book is written according to the canons of aesthetic or artistic logic.

This affirmative report of the radical suburb does not imply that we are thoroughly happy with suburban playfulness. The playful mentality, as we shall see, has pathological possibilities, springing from both negligence and guilt. People can suffer from it. The nonplayful can be set aside by a ruthless apartheid, and the playful themselves can be victimized in their unawareness. But there is such a thing as the act of transcendence, the process of listening to one's own story, and consequently the ability to have some purchase on one's direction. Hopefully that act can forestall and eliminate some of the negative elements that we detect in a generally exciting and constructive moral development within the suburbs.

J. B. O.
F. P. N.

University of Southern California
Los Angeles, California

Part I

————————

THE SHAPE
OF THE RADICAL SUBURB

Chapter 1

THE INVISIBILITY
OF THE RADICAL SUBURB

THIS IS A BOOK about American character—more particularly, about a transformation in the character of the American middle class that can only be described as radical. We are aware, of course, that the word "radical" hardly seems to fit the configuration of Boy Scout troops, supermarkets, potluck suppers, men's groups, Little League tournaments, station wagons, campers, pieties, and pale conservative manners that are the manna of life in middle-class suburbia. Radicalism seems, rather, to be the property of rebellious youth, who conspire with the disenfranchised minorities of the central city and in frightening ways find common cause with disillusioned anarchists of the far right. But our point is that the most revolutionary population in American life is going unidentified. Forces have been playing on the American middle class in the last fifty years that have succeeded in creating a new culturally revolutionary class. Just how this has taken place, what kind of plot has developed in the shadow of the shopping plaza, and what are the implications of this radicalism for some major institutions and activities of American life: these are the concerns of this book.

Such a book must assume that it makes sense to speak about the character of American middle-class suburbanites

—that is, about social character. When, almost two hundred years ago, Crèvecoeur asked his famous question, "Who then is the American, this new man?" he did not bother to argue elaborately about his premise that Americans did constitute a new breed and that they did exhibit shared character traits. Crèvecoeur had to start someplace, and he chose to start with what interested him: describing the fascinating habits of the renegade American culture. Crèvecoeur's procedure allowed him to share a number of intuitions about this culture without self-consciously having to make these explicit in terms of social theory, and he was able to make an important contribution. Admittedly, he ignored some theoretical issues that can no longer so easily be swept out of sight, but with some modifications his procedure is ours. We are assuming that, regardless of difficult issues surrounding the fundamental definition of social character, there are important things to say about the changing atmosphere of feeling in American life. Rather than give the most attention to interminable in-house debates about social character, we will simply describe what we see within suburban life-styles.

We do have a responsibility, though, to state at least our working definition of "social character." Clearly, "character" is not intended to be synonymous with "personality," the latter being the whole complex of factors that form an individual's life-style. Nor do we intend social character to mean all the traits that are shared widely in a particular group (such as, for example, our national habit of driving on the right side of the road, or of eating peas with a fork and not with the much more logical spoon). Social character, instead, has to do with the perspectives and feelings shared by persons in groups—the ways people experience their environment, leading to broad consensuses about appropriate feelings, beliefs, and behavior. Each individual in the group does not have to exhibit traits of the social character in an identical way, because, of course, no two persons interact with their culture in exactly the same way. But individuals in groups are affected by similar forces and make common adjustments. They tend to come up with common commitments to values, common feelings, common modes of behavior, and common ways of interpreting their experiences.

Our biases are frankly with the approach to social character currently being worked out by Erik H. Erikson and Robert Jay Lifton, both of whom are skeptical about the value of using the words "personality" and "character." These words suggest fixity, whereas what we are observing in the American situation is flux. Erikson prefers to use the word "identity" when he points to changing patterns of perspectives and feelings, and Lifton uses the term "self-process" to suggest flow. Lifton argues that the idea of a stable social character is associated with traditional cultures in which man's relationship to his institutions is relatively unchanging, which is certainly not the case in America today. He observes that basic ideas of selfhood change, often radically, within a continuous psychic process.[1]

Our linguistic sympathies are with Lifton and Erikson, and whatever is said here about social character will presuppose their clarifying arguments. Nevertheless, we have not chosen to drop the word "character" from our vocabulary, because we are accustomed to it and believe it to be capable of a good and proper salvation.

In speaking about the social character of the suburb, we should also be as clear as possible concerning the boundaries of our investigation. Obviously, the word "suburb" has geographical connotations, evoking images of the residential communities that surround the downtowns of urban America. The images are of relative affluence and of that peculiar phenomenon, the anticity: tracts designed with a clever use of architecture, trees, lawns, and lakes to give the impression of "a little bit of country, even here." As we use the term, though, the radical suburb is not so much a place as it is a social grouping. It refers to the middle and upper middle class of urban Americans, most of whom do live in suburban communities, but many of whom live in urban apartment complexes and in affluent residential pockets within the central city. The radical suburb also abounds in rural and university communities, in which business and professional families are able to maintain life-styles that are almost indistinguishable from their urban and suburban counterparts.

At best, it seems ironical to speak about suburban America as radical. At worst, it appears to be an indefensible act of journalistic trickery—a sensationalist reversal of the usual meaning of terms. The picture of the suburb that is commonly shared, even among perceptive observers, is one of conformism. Suburban tracts provide shelter for families who have emerged victorious in the struggle for civilized comforts, and suburbanites are engaged in a brutal, albeit sophisticated, struggle to wall off their treelined enclaves from the decaying urban acreage. They are the conservative vertebrae of an inflexible body politic that repeatedly proves itself unable to respond creatively to accumulating environmental poisons. They fill the churches long after theologian-prophets have proclaimed the death of God, and they stand absolutely rigid when "The Star-spangled Banner" is played. Radical? Revolutionary?

Our impression is that the radicality of the suburb is largely hidden to American eyes, even though this radicality is pervasive, its symptoms everywhere. One reason for this strange state of perceptual affairs is that the ways in which Americans have described their national character have become routine and frozen to the point where departures from what we expect to find in suburban character are virtually unrecognizable. Like parents who refuse to recognize discontinuities in the transition of their offspring from childhood to maturity, observers have persisted in describing American character in ways that are reminiscent of the diaries and papers of early travelers, settlers, and journalistic prophets. It is this remarkable descriptive continuity that leads Seymour Lipset to conclude that there must be something stable in the American character.[2] But John Dewey's explanation seems more persuasive: Americans of the later industrial society, he argues, tend to describe themselves and their moral obligations in terms appropriate to a stable, highly individualistic, agrarian culture. Although they are experiencing a cultural transition of massive proportions, Americans are often not able to discern what is happening to themselves because they think of themselves in terms of images that no longer apply. Dewey, of course, was trying to call his fellow citizens to a more scientific, pragmatic style of life, but he was also urging them to revise their perceptions of culture in order that they might reckon with significant cultural changes.

Barriers to Perception: Routine Descriptions of American Character

At least two distinct models of American character have emerged victorious in the long history of people-watching in the United States, and these continue to shape our perceptions in ways that make it difficult to notice radical changes of suburban style. One of the models describes the American as an individualist and as freedom-loving, while the other sees him as a conformist and as one who values equality. Although the models to some extent represent contradictory and incompatible assessments of what has developed as a national character, they can also be represented in a more dialectic manner as contrasting styles that have assumed more or less importance at different moments in American history.[3] For our purposes, though, the models are also potentially conservative forces because they freeze what we look for in American character and provide the images within which we habitually describe American character change.

Those who emphasize the individualist model are likely to trace origins of American character to the demanding days of migration to the New World or to the conquest of the Western wilderness. They argue that less adventurous spirits were screened out in the process of facing frontier hardships and that, further, frontiers demanded a high degree of resourcefulness and fortitude. Thomas Jefferson gave the individualist concept of American character its classic formulation in his contention that America's non-hierarchical society depended for its vitality on the independent farmer. Jefferson's model American thus was of the Davy Crockett variety—independent, self-reliant, individualistic, resourceful.

The alternative model—that of the American as conformist and equalitarian—can be found at least as early as the Jacksonian era, when Alexis de Tocqueville caustically observed that he knew of no country where there was "so little independence of mind and freedom of discussion as in America." De Tocqueville viewed American habits through aristocratic biases, but his views were repeated over and over by visitors in the late eighteenth and nineteenth centuries. Americans were seen to exhibit "acute sensitiveness to opinion," "fear of singularity," and the propensity to "dream noble deeds" without acting on them.

Descriptions of the American as either freedom-loving or equalitarian continue into our own period, the shifting emphases apparently reflecting changing social conditions. Writers of the depression years, for example, bewailed the decline of equalitarian sensitivities and the rise of an individualistic, competitive, achievement-oriented culture—a decline that denied New Deal experimentalism its needed foundations. Karen Horney's *The Neurotic Personality of Our Time,* for example, vividly chronicled the American anxieties over economic success that are bred within the competitive American economy. And W. L. Warner, Harold Laski, and Robert Lynd argued that giant corporations, competition, and monopolistic markets were destroying the foundations of American democracy.

The war-fed affluence of the 1950's, however, brought a number of American character studies that argued in precisely the opposite way. William H. Whyte's *The Organization Man,* for example, claimed that America's achievement ethic and spirit of Protestant individualism were being destroyed under the impact of a new social ethic, which he defined as making the group a "source of creativity," and encouraging "a belief in the application of science to achieve belongingness." In *The Lonely Crowd,* David Riesman agreed with Whyte. He described two types of Americans: (1) the inner-directed man, whose values are deeply internalized and whose style of living is individualistic; and (2) the other-directed man, whose views change as prevailing peer attitudes shift, and whose style of living is conformist. Riesman claimed that the inner-directed man has been superseded in the twentieth century by the other-directed personality—a momentous historical change that he associated with developments in population growth.

In other words, observers of Yankee culture have disagreed about which traits are predominant in American character, but they have persistently agreed in their disagreement. They have agreed that the American is either a conformist, an individualist, or both, depending on the circumstances. A corollary to this agreement is that the American social scene, in its manners, politics, education, and industry, has been characterized by the clash or interaction of the individualist and conformist styles. Our most socially disruptive issues have been identified within this spectrum: the individual against the collective; freedom against social controls; the demand for equality of opportunity; the demand for various forms of economic welfare. Our national history can be and has been charted as a pendulum wildly swinging between the poles of freedom and equality. Extremes of freedom have given rise to exploitation of the politically and economically weak, which in turn has created pressures for equalitarian schemes to correct the most obvious abuses. But equality-creating projects have encouraged totalitarianism and a dull uniformity, which in turn have spurred movements to demand the restoration of freedoms.

The interesting point is that radicality in America has largely been defined on this same scale, although we do have an equally strong practice of branding as radical persons who hold fervently to *any* particular belief system. The American radical is stereotyped as one who demands either more freedom or more equality, his identifying mark as a radical being the utter dogmatism and inflexibility with which he pursues libertarian and/or equalitarian causes. His radicality assumes a negative form when his dogmatism lashes out with harsh judgments about the absence of either freedom or equality in our "sick society." Even when radicality assumes forms that are not on their face political—for example, the radicality of the religious zealot—on the American scene the issue of freedom and equality seems inevitably to rear up. Conservative Christian dogmatism is hardly distinguishable in the eyes of many from the liberty-preaching politics of the far right. And it seems just as difficult to tell the difference between the religious ethics of the liberal theologian and those of other liberal strategists on behalf of various assortments of libertarian or equalitarian causes.

The new radicality of the suburb, which this book will describe, though, is hidden to American eyes, just because what is happening within the middle class is too novel to be described easily with phrases drawn from traditional descriptions of the American character. What is happening in the suburb is not the evolution of a passion for equality—for the reform of a defunct welfare system, the extension of open housing, the strengthening of equal employment opportunity, or even the naked enforcement of conformities. Nor is it the evolution of a passion for liberty—a resurgence of the privatism or individualism that has appeared in American character studies as either the unwelcome fruit of a competitive capitalism or as a fragile virtue persistently threatened by America's vigorous conformist spirit.

The new radicalization of the American suburb, rather, is the fruit of a cultural revolution. Such revolutions can often proceed invisibly within a society, particularly when they do not directly threaten the political *status quo*. They are recognizable after the fact, when their transformation is well established and when, of necessity, a vocabulary arises that is appropriate to the emergent cultural forms. Our failure to chart and to appreciate the new radicality of the suburb rests on the ironical situation that the most extreme forms of social change may be the most invisible, simply because they challenge our habits of observation too severely.

The paradox of the suburb is almost too stark to be perceived: the Neanderthal suburbanite turns out to be a cultural radical. While we have been wailing about the inactivity of the middle class in championing the cause of the powerless and the not-fully-liberated, the suburbanite has been busy with his own agenda, which in its own way is profoundly revolutionay. The failure of the middle class to find political solutions for the era of urban crises may well prove to be the Achilles' heel of the suburb, the source of its fall. But meanwhile the suburb is intent on carrying out its own revolution, a cultural radicalization that seems to be rendering the familiar expectations concerning American character the ultimate insult—ignoring them.

Barriers to Perception: Negative Myths of the Suburb

Another reason that the new radicality of the suburb is so largely hidden to American eyes is that our perception of the middle class has been shaped by a number of powerful myths that have become so much a part of our common sense that they go unacknowledged. They do not necessarily breed distortions of what is there in the suburb. They are not phantoms that need to be destroyed so that the mind might more accurately mirror suburban reality. The myths do shape our perceptions of the suburb and they do make it unlikely that we will recognize sharp breaks in suburban tradition. But they are myths that serve worthy purposes and should not be faddishly branded as unnecessary or outmoded.

The trouble with the several myths is that they are mutually reinforcing. They conspire in a totalitarian way to close off debate about the suburb, because they agree in the diagnosis that the suburb is a place of conservative comfort, escape, reaction, and protected advantage. Thus they contribute to the decay of community pride that currently afflicts suburbia and that was painfully bared by the Black Power movements of the 1960's. When Negroes began to celebrate black identity—to chant "Black is beautiful"—there were unmistakable signs that their ability to celebrate identity was not equally possessed by the white middle class. Buffeted by charges of white racism and institutional violence, suburbanites discovered that their self-image was largely negative. White, Anglo-Saxon Protestant (WASP) became a term of derision, or what is worse, a term utilized by suburbanites to cartoon their own middle-class failures. The middle class, when faced with the necessity of defining itself over and against the black community, found that its mythology was negative and that its springs of collective pride were dried at their sources.

On the one hand, Marxist mythology had affected suburban self-understanding more than might have been imagined possible within a highly anti-Communist era. Schooled in the views of political analysts who had been affected in the 1930's by the Marxist diagnoses of capitalist ills and ministered to by preachers who had been to seminary in the days of a flowering Christian socialism, suburbanites appropriated a Marxist self-image in spite of themselves. The suburb appeared as an exploitative phenomenon. It boasted treelined streets, well-developed parks, efficient city services, and enforced building codes when just the opposite was the case for the lower-income populations of the central city. Like a greedy hawk, the middle class drew its lifeblood from the central city but carried its income to the shady lanes of the suburb without paying its fair share for services used in the process. Absentee landlords and suburban institutions owned the city slums and expected the city's middle-class government to look the other way when building codes and safety standards were ignored. Ghetto schools languished as the city's property taxes declined, while suburban communities lobbied in state legislatures to maintain their advantage. Thus, the more socially aware members of the middle class began to see that the nicety of the suburb was bought at a high price and that it had to be understood as the prize of a class victory.

The Marxist image of the suburb was strangely buttressed by another myth more endemic to the American situation, one that has come to be known as the "agrarian myth." Rooted in the Jeffersonian fear of urbanization and in the correlate glorification of virgin territory and agriculture, this myth has had a double edge. It has reinforced the widely held idea that the suburb with its trees and lawns is a good place to raise children, as over against the concrete jungles of the city. But it also has produced the notion that the city is where the thorny problems are, where the action is, and therefore where responsible people should be engaged. Urban universities, far from envying their suburban, rural counterparts, have boasted about the realistic education to be secured in the laboratory of urban problem-solving. They have organized centers of urban studies and have looked with disdain upon graduates who ignore the problems of urban America and who pursue their fortunes in the suburbs. The suburbs have been viewed as the place where intelligent people go to ossify, and where they go to escape from the really important issues of American society. In the 1960's, when black militants urged white people to minister to their own sicknesses in white society, suburbanites could think of few appropriate responses other than to take urban sight-seeing tours or to import the city into the suburb by means of movies and panels of urban actionists. Passively, the suburbanite agreed with his urban brother, who was himself under the spell of the agrarian myth, in imagining that the suburb was retreat. The suburbanite did not think of counterattacking by pointing to his own middle-class revolution, or of arguing that he was himself engaged in a culturally radical process.

Most recently, another myth—that of the "urban organism" or the "urban system"—has conspired to conceal the radicality of the suburb. This is a liberal, university-bred myth, nurtured by the astonishing contribution that systems analysis has made to the conceptualization of urban problems. It views the metropolitan area as a totality, every part interacting with every other part, solutions to urban ills demanding regional approaches. In effect, urbanologists urge that one ought not to speak about the suburb because to do so implies that the suburb can logically be distinguished from the metropolitan whole. To describe suburban life-styles is to encourage a political climate in which the middle class can more easily divorce its own interests from those of the wider population. For pragmatic reasons, we ought to refuse to carve the metropolis into competitive parts, each warring for its own advantage. The myth of the urban organism encourages us to draw away from the suburb and to comprehend its life patterns within the total urban crisis. The suburb emerges as a place that contributes to urban problems, but as yet supplies few answers. Again, its image is negative; the myth of the urban organism tends finally to legitimate both the agrarian myth and the Marxist myth.

Myths of the American suburb are not lies, and in fact uncover important dimensions of American experience. Their fault is not in commission, but in omission. They simply do not encourage us to recognize other dimensions, the acknowledgment of which completes the description of suburban America. There is no one way to view the suburb, and no one myth is sufficient to characterize its multifaceted existence. The chapters that follow are intended as balances to the negative myths of the suburb, their point being that the suburbs are doing a job that is quite novel and fresh in the Western world. If the suburb is resistant to the solution of urban decay, it is also nurturing a mentality and mode of behavior that constitute a watershed happening within the history of Western man.

Chapter 2

_____

EXPANSIVE MAN

WE FIRST STARTED to notice the radical suburb in the mid-1950's, just at the time when middle-class America was flagellating itself for its other-directedness, conformism, and gray-flannel manners. William Whyte's organization man was a team man, and Whyte was not at all certain in 1956 that America could survive economically and culturally when entrusted to the care of such an individual. A secondary detail in *The Organization Man* caught our attention, however, and made us wonder whether Whyte had stumbled on to a suburban happening that was very important but only awkwardly explained by his own thesis about the organizational personality. He observed that organization man had the capacity to move casually from one church to another. The mobility of the suburbanite had not spurred a dogmatic denominational loyalty designed to maintain an element of stability in a highly unstable life pattern. Instead, the suburbanite did not hesitate to change his denomination when there was no church of his faith in the immediate neighborhood, when his own church seemed to be mediocre, or when he was attracted by the ministry of a particular preacher. In spite of his apparent need for cultural constants, organization man had become an inveterate church shopper.

What struck us was how different this church-shopping style was from that to which our own Puritan and Catholic families had accustomed us and from that which American piety has tended to make normative. It has traditionally been a wrenching experience to "leave the church," and most families, if pressed, could probably recall only one or two times when religious ties had been severed, or minds fundamentally changed about religious beliefs. Organization man, however, was a floater, and it apparently made little difference whether his church was Congregational, Church of Christ, Presbyterian, Unitarian, or Baptist.

Whyte explained that the various churches tend to lose their identity in the process of meeting the demand for a common American religion, and that the suburbanite is looking for an experience of community more than anything else.[4] His explanation, though, seemed overplayed and foreign to our experience of the suburb. Sharp differences do indeed exist among the atmospheres and practices of churches; and if organization man is casual about his religious connections, he apparently is able to derive satisfaction from worship services and symbols that have little in common with one another. At least with regard to his religious life, he is fickle to a degree that is astonishing from the viewpoint of orthodox expectations.

Like so many popularized accounts of American character, Whyte's study grew out of a particular time and place. Our memory of organization man's churchgoing habits, however, has been revived in recent years and we have had to conclude that Whyte's odd, unsatisfying comments about church attendance were really quite perceptive, even though he had no way of recognizing the radicality of the process that he was observing. During the past few years, his observations appear mild, because middle-class religious eclecticism now ranges far beyond the practice of dabbling with various denominational loyalties. It is not uncommon now to discover Zen Christians among the offspring of suburbia—students who may hold leadership positions in church-sponsored associations, but who nevertheless find meaning in Zen Buddhist devotional literature and exercises and often add incense and the Confucian practice of I Ching to their religious rituals. Both they and their parents may find excitement and satisfaction in astrological and numerological studies, yoga, and mystical meditation, while experiencing few tensions with their Western faith. They do not seem to be troubled by the absence of coherence in their experience or in their understanding of ultimates. Instead, they are playful with religious symbols.

One explanation, of course, is Whyte's: that suburbia is a faddish place; its religious pace, energized by the suburban thirst for community, is set by whatever catches the popular fancy. From Whyte's perspective, suburbia is a "cute culture," where the most fundamental beliefs recommend themselves because they can offer "a new twist" that "seems to be catching on." But a more interesting hypothesis is that the religious style we have observed is an aspect of a much larger and more radical character transformation, which—when acknowledged—can be seen almost everywhere in middle-class America.

That such a hypothesis is worth investigating is confirmed by a number of perceptive writers who have noticed the coming of a new social character type, all of whom believe this development to be decisive in the evolution of Western man. Philip Rieff, for example, speaks of the arrival on the scene of a new character ideal that succeeds the three ideals that previously had dominated Western civilization: political man, religious man, and economic man. The new ideal, he claims, is psychological man, "a child, not of nature, but of technology." Psychological man is uncommitted to the public life, antiheroic, shrewd, calculating his satisfactions and dissatisfactions, and looking upon belief systems as sins to be avoided. According to Rieff, "the psychological man neither lives by the ideal of might nor the ideal of right which confused his ancestors, political man and religious man. Psychological man lives by the ideal of insight—practical, experimental insight leading to the mastery of his own personality." [5] He turns away from the Western ideal of concern for the salvation of others and adopts a more Oriental interest in the enrichment of experience through self-contemplative manipulation. The self becomes the last frontier to be conquered.

Rieff's discussion concerning the new character type, strangely enough, grows out of his preoccupation with the Freudian philosophy of culture and not out of a disciplined study of Western social behavior. In his book *The Triumph of the Therapeutic,* in which psychological man is described at great length, Rieff implies that psychological man will arrive on the scene because he represents a culmination of Freud's estimate of the direction of cultural evolution. In this respect, Rieff's comments take on an abstract air; they constitute a moral chronicle based essentially on an outline of a philosophy of history.[6]

From a vastly different perspective and in a far different mood, Rieff's announcement of psychological man is reinforced by the observations of Robert Jay Lifton, a Yale psychologist. Lifton speaks about the appearance of "a set of psychological patterns characteristic of contemporary life, which are creating a new kind of man—a 'protean man.' " [7] The name, of course, is derived from the Greek mythological figure Proteus, who was capable of altering his shape at will—from wild boar, to dragon, to earth, to maiden, to flood. What he could not or would not do, though, was to accept the role of prophet that would accompany the commitment to a single form.

The protean style, Lifton says, is "characterized by an interminable series of experiments and explorations—some shallow, some profound—each of which may be readily abandoned in favor of still new psychological quests." [8] The style should not be viewed as pathological, although it is far from being an unmixed blessing. It ought to be accepted as one of the functional patterns of our era—a reshaping of life-styles that to some extent has proved stable and that reaches to all parts of human experience, including the political and the sexual.

Lifton's discovery of protean man was after the fact. Unlike Rieff, Lifton was not looking for a new life-process ideal because he had seen a star in the sky (that is, because he had a theory that enabled him to predict the emergence of such an ideal). Lifton found protean man in his studies of Japanese and Chinese youth, particularly in his reconstruction of the personal history of one middle-class Japanese boy. The boy, in the space of a few years, had moved in a chameleon manner through the characterological styles of fiery Japanese patriot, eager exponent of American culture, scholar, intellectual Marxist, Christian, Japanese cultural enthusiast, Communist, dissipator, and conservative businessman. Lifton found the same protean pattern among Chinese youth, regardless of their associations with thought reform, and then he proceeded to recognize the pattern as a worldwide phenomenon. Obvious differences among protean life-styles in various regions existed, but clear-cut similarities also suggested that an important transition in life-style was broadly under way.

Whether or not Lifton has actually discovered a worldwide characterological revolution is beyond the scope of this study. What is remarkable is the cultural significance of his observations, confirmed in an odd way by Rieff's analysis of psychological man and by our own observations that a change in American character is occurring in the suburbs. If the hypothesis is valid, and we believe it is, then we need to reverse our conventional wisdom about the revolutions and radicalities within American society. We have habitually pictured the revolutions of our era in terms of the hard symbols of confrontation: black against white, young against old, rich against poor, West against East, conservative against liberal. These confrontations are terribly important. But the cultural revolution is a soft phenomenon: the silent radicalizing of persons through the development of life-process styles that are freshly novel in the Western world.

Who is the suburban radical? What is he like? The most appropriate way to describe him is to say that he is an *expansive personality*—an expansive man, devoted to the process of enlarging his experience, enlarging the number of perspectives within which his world can be perceived and felt, enlarging awareness of his own sensual and intellectual capabilities, and enlarging his ability to be playful with ideas and possessions.

When we speak about the suburb, we are not suggesting that everyone who lives in the American suburb is a radical, nor even that the overall atmosphere of the suburb is as yet radical. The point is, rather, that there are forces at work that lead, in an irreversible manner, in this direction, and that a growing number of suburbanites comprise a revolutionary cadre in American life. For the present, the radical will have to share his territory with neighbors who are not very sympathetic to his cause, and his take-over of middle-income tracts will have to remain on a house-by-house, person-by-person basis. In fact, it would be helpful to resist the temptation to think about the radical suburb as a collection of individuals. A far more prudent and realistic practice would be to think in terms of tendencies, directions, and styles of life that are more or less evident in the character process of suburbanites.

What is also apparent is that this cultural revolution is hardly at all a matter of generation gaps, but that gray-haired bankers and their rebellious sons are united as allies in the cause. Clearly, the language and practice of the youth culture differs considerably from that of adults, just as children's games everywhere are distinct, but radical styles do not belong to any age group as a private preserve. Middle-class students are caught up by the same forces that are affecting their parents. If anything, middle-class youth can best be understood as forerunners, experimenting with styles in a freer way than is socially possible in suburbia, yet actualizing life patterns learned at their mothers' net-stockinged knees.

The coming of expansive man to the American suburb marks the end of an epoch and the beginning of a different way of being human. The style of life represented by expansive man has its foundation and development within Western thought, and one can find Western philosophers and theologians who have come very close to describing the expansive characterological ideal. But at least in America, the ideal has not until recently assumed power as a revolutionary myth, nor has it described a style of life that is daily being generated by a large number of persons.

The Self as Process

At the most abstract level, middle-class radicalization is experienced as the emergence of a process understanding of what it is to be human. Western thought has encouraged persons to think of themselves as entities rather than processes, beings rather than evolving experiences. Cynically, a predominant form of this thinking of man might be called "the ghost in the box" concept—the idea that each of us is a self that happens to possess a body, that takes on various character traits over time, and that expresses itself by means of a variety of activities.

In the Christian community, the notion was expressed in the popular belief that persons have souls that are eternal, where bodies and personality characteristics are finite and relative. In Western philosophy, heavily influenced by the Platonic-Christian understanding of man, Descartes described the traditional view characteristically, albeit crudely. The self is an entity with a characteristic identity: it is free, not subject to the assorted laws under which the rest of nature groans.

In Western thought, David Hume seemed almost to be pushing a coarse joke when he announced that he could find no reason whatsoever to accept the idea of an eternal soul or self. Whenever he attempted to observe his own life in action, all he could find was a number of sensations, perceptions, and passions. For Hume, then, if we chose to use the word "self," we ought to identify it with this succession of experiences rather than with the ghost in the box. His view of the self was later echoed by American pragmatists such as William James and John Dewey, who viewed the self as a process actually constituted in the experience of solving problems.

In the suburb, Hume's coarse joke no longer sounds very funny, and for a growing number of suburbanites it can be accepted as commonsensical. Whether or not this development in self-understanding is connected with the secularization of American society remains an interesting issue to explore. But the fact remains that we are less and less interested in thinking about ourselves as eternal beings, and more and more interested in calculating a life process that includes entertaining, enriching, and shocking experiences. If asked for their opinions, most suburbanites, in or out of the churches, would probably not care to defend the village atheist's denial of "the existence of the soul." Their behavior, though, would belie their expressed opinions. Their time is not spent in caring for the soul's state of health, but in playing golf, swinging from party to party, playing with astrology and ski equipment, and occasionally going to church. The usual question is not whether life constitutes a meaningful whole; it is whether the family has a rich, interesting schedule lined up for the next few weeks.

Those who look to the expansive man for startling new

and unheard-of ideas on the problem of self will find little. Those who look to him for practical guidance on how to lead the soulless life may find abundant help. The great contribution of the expansive style is more practical than theoretical, because its origins bend it in that direction. The suburban concept of the self as a process of experiences did not blossom from any breakthrough in the long Western debate about the nature of the self, and it certainly did not arise from a refutation of orthodox religious arguments. The source is, rather, in a cultural revolution that deprives persons of stable models of the self, and even the taste for these models, and focuses interest on the process of change instead.

Suburbanites, to put it bluntly, find it hard to identify with the angels that are enshrined in their churches' stained-glass windows; on reflection, they are more apt to see themselves in the kinetic art that they occasionally enjoy at local galleries. This, of course, is an art form that will not stand still. Using complicated electronic mechanisms, it creates an unending sequence of illusions, moving objects, and geometrical arrangements, at times producing a feeling of vertigo. Or the suburbanites may find themselves represented in the momentum games currently being produced for the suburban market. The Wheelo game, for example, is a plaything in every sense of the word. It has no object, no ultimate challenge, no rules; it is merely to play with and to observe. Another game has six balls strung in a line from a rectangular frame. When a ball is tapped and hits the next, energy is transferred through the whole set. The process may begin by the player's tapping any one of the balls, or any set, so that the possibility of new arrangements for energy transfer appears unlimited. In neither of these games is there a moment when anyone finally wins, nor is there a way to conclude that anyone is a better or worse player. The games consist in a potentially endless process; the worth and satisfaction are in the doing rather than in the achievement of a goal.

Of course, there are powerful precedents for this process view of selfhood in the Biblical faith as well as in the lives of saints and reformers. But in a strange way, the expansive experience of the self is also reminiscent of the Buddhist doctrine of *anatman*. The term *anatman* is usually translated as "soullessness," but Buddhism is really not interested in denying the existence of the personality or the soul in an empirical sense. What is claimed, though, is that the concept of the soul is irrelevant. Far more interesting is an approach to understanding the self which looks upon the individual as *santana,* a stream of interconnected experiences. Even when Buddhism extends the life-span within a series of reincarnations, a doctrine of eternal soul is not assumed, only a continuity of experiences that are mysteriously held together.[9]

The surprising parallel between the expansive and the Buddhist concepts of the self as process is potentially explosive within Western culture. It partially explains why suburbanites are often bedazzled by Zen Buddhists and by the writings of Eastern mystics. More important, it opens an experiential wedge through which previously foreign perspectives and feelings might flow into the suburban landscape. In many ways, the radicalization of the suburb could also be understood as the Easternization of the American middle class—a possibility that has not as yet fully been acknowledged, but one that we shall have to explore in any future study of American character.

Experience as the Highest Good

The practical acceptance of the self as process rather than as an entity greatly heightens the importance of sustaining a round of interesting, intensive experiences. Indeed, the expansion of experience becomes an end in itself to be achieved. Expansive man's style of life becomes a process of planning and executing a kaleidoscope of happenings marked by different tones and qualities and demanding contrasting degrees of emotional output. Times of quietness (art books, cheese and crackers in front of the fireplace) alternate with moments of controlled gentility (cocktail parties and gourmet cooking), moments of gaudy benevolence (Assistance League benefits), boisterous outbursts (wild cheers for a favorite politician), tests of prowess (the shooting range and neighborhood bowling leagues), feelings of sophistication (two patron's tickets to the city symphony), times scheduled for health (yoga, jogging, TV exercises), savage emotions ("being honest" in the neighborhood sensitivity group), and on and on. The expansive man likes to furnish his home and his office in ways that heighten his experience through interesting textures, colors, and bold innovations which either entrance or offend. He is faithfully attended by magazines that suggest decorating schemes, landscaping designs, family projects, and menus that self-consciously portray and stimulate desired atmospheres. And he is serviced by what can only be called the Experience Industry: restaurants that simulate visits to almost every point on the globe and almost every moment in the past; beauty pageants; topless bars; sports events; stores that seem more intent on creating moods than in selling their products.

At first glance, the radical preoccupation with experience looks like debauchery, a hedonistic extravaganza. It also looks exhausting and a little pointless, too mundane to be really exciting, yet too exciting to be like *Life with Father*. On closer examination, though, the word "hedonism" seems out of place. Hedonism aims at a finished product: the state of maximized pleasure. But suburban expansiveness is less concerned about pleasure than about enlarging experience, being both interesting and interested, luxuriating in an environment that is capable of enriching the personality, being open to persons and things. The spirit of the radical's expansiveness is well expressed in the painting *Looking Back* by the Viennese artist Erich Brauer. Its central figure is a curiously green man with a large ear growing from his trousers and holes in his shoes. In his own interpretation, Brauer asks, "Why not have an extra ear in one's trousers, to hear better and different things?" And why not have holes in shoes, because "it makes the feet more interesting"? [10]

That the expansive style is not simply hedonism is also shown by the fact that the radical does not retreat from rigorous, demanding commitments. He often devotes a burdensome amount of time to community organizations, including churches. He may be a vestryman in the local Episcopal church, or a Presbyterian ruling elder, or a council member for the Y.M.C.A. He is occasionally active in politics, even to the point of assuming the ascetic disciplines of radical political communities. And he may be found spending hours figuring out studies on ESP, trying Zen puzzles, or plodding through technical material on astrology. He is not drawn to the esoteric to the exclusion of other areas of intellectual discipline, however, and he is rapidly turning adult education programs into a booming suburban business. The expansive man, when told that his intensive style shows a dabbling character devoid of serious commitment, can only disagree, because from his perspective, his style is motivated by an urge to be fully involved in his surroundings. His is not a serene existence, like that cultivated in Epicurus' famous, although often misunderstood, garden.

The experience-hungry style of the suburban radical is better interpreted as an attempt to live as an artist works: concerned with colors and contrasts and ultimately with the beauty of sharing in the artistic process. The style is not passive; the suburban radical does not let himself be formed by the titillating products of the suburban market. He is more aggressive—more impressed with the possibility of surrounding himself with an atmosphere of his own invention. Enclosed in the suburban environment, which places a premium on manufactured articles and on the rearrangement of natural objects, he enthusiastically accepts his role as creator of or contributor to reality. As a moral artist, expansive man refuses to relate to his world as a spectator. His experimentalism with experience constitutes the way he tries out various life possibilities, and the way he pragmatically pieces together an environment (or world) that is satisfying and mature.

Eclecticism

The fact, then, is that the suburban radical cannot believe that his whole life should be devoted to a particular dogma or cause, or that the rest of his life should be similar to the present. Almost in spite of himself, the radical is impatient with persons whose style is one of consistent and dedicated loyalty to a single cause. It is not that he disagrees with them. In fact, he admires them for their personal sacrifice and often feels unworthy in their presence. When expansive man goes to the Y.M.C.A. board meeting, for example, he is puzzled by his neighbor's failure to see the humor involved in planning powwows and in reciting vows about "the beauty of the Great Spirit's work." But he is glad for the neighbor's involvement, because at least the neighbor will do much of the dirty work in preparing for the next powow. At the vestry meeting, expansive man is entranced by his neighbor's unshakable faith and secretly brands himself as a hypocrite and wishes that he could devote himself totally to a life-giving set of beliefs. But at the same time, his involved, consistent neighbor seems far too serious and too impressed with the rightness of the beliefs that inspire his involvement. Consistency appears to be anachronistic, a stale reminder of yesterday, starved for the richness that a freer style might produce.

The expansive man has not as yet learned to accept his own playfulness with beliefs as a positive good, but he knows that he cannot return ever again to the virgin territory of consistency. He has crossed the bridge and has lost the toll that would enable him to return. The theologian Søren Kierkegaard's dictum that "purity of heart is to will one thing" belongs to a vision of self-integration that grows increasingly weak. The expansive man, frankly, feels more identity with the writings of another existentialist, Jean-Paul Sartre, who conveys his uneasiness with Marxists who cannot understand that the revolution is a finite, changeable phenomenon. Expansiveness is restless, in search of commitments that are interesting, and capable of appreciating conflicting points of view.

The expansive man, in short, is incorrigibly eclectic. One of the graduate students with whom we have contact may serve as an example. This student, an intelligent young lady, was raised in a Conservative Jewish family and continues to feel strongly, yet mainly nostalgically, about her Jewish heritage. For many years she has identified herself as a Zionist, although this is a loyalty that she flips in and out of. In her college years, however, she found meaning in Reinhold Niebuhr's Christian theology of immanence and transcendence, and in the image of Jesus as "the man for others," but she also moved periodically in and out of atheistic stages. Likewise, she and a friend found great satisfaction at a Zen retreat center in the mountains near San Francisco. (The friend, incidentally, recently demonstrated as a radical against the president of his university, then two weeks later asked the president for help in securing a position in the plastics industry.) She also moved through a series of majors during her four undergraduate years: prelaw to political science to urban studies to speech to religion.

She was simultaneously an active leader in student government and a plotter of student revolution. She enjoys the security of her family's affluence, while romanticizing the happy peasant life. And she has been known, in the confines of one essay, to argue vigorously as an exponent of both absolute moral principles and moral relativity.

The point is not that the expansive man is intellectually fickle. Eclecticism does not necessarily grow from instability, but may grow out of the habit of mind that looks for what different points of view have to offer and that is aware of how arbitrary belief systems can be. Furthermore, eclecticism may be associated with an acute sense of beauty that finds in the multiplicity of world views an entrée to the infinite potentiality for rich human creativity. To his suburban neighbors, the expansive man may look like an intellectual cad. But the expansive man does not see what is so virtuous about being consistent and may even find more virtue in enlarging his experience and commitments within a multiplicity of directions. To the amazement of serious observers of the suburban mentality, the whole notion that a person's intellectual and religious life ought to form an organic unity is being broadly questioned. What used to be the cardinal sin in the suburban classroom—arguing in a self-contradictory manner—now tends to be dismissed with a shrug of the shoulders.

Expansive man's puzzling eclecticism can be understood as a strange, indirect victory for the philosopher Immanuel Kant. Working out of the context of Christian piety, he believed that persons become moral heroes when they become masters unto themselves, self-legislators, always in control of the moral laws they are applying to their own behavior. The eclectic individual thereby assumes heroic proportions in the Kantian frame of reference. He is liberated and in control of his own commitments, not subject even to the demand for logical consistency. The expansive style is able to work within traditional belief systems and religious communities, yet is always detached and can enjoy competitive points of view because it is never totally controlled by any one view. Expansive styles can comprehend tribal superstitions and Christian theology, can take both seriously; but the expansive man is always the one to dictate the degree of involvement that is appropriate to each at the moment.

This liberation and detachment is probably, at least in part, a logical entailment of expansive man's Western faith background. The Catholic faith, for example, has always affirmed a species of cultural and moral relativism by maintaining that God reveals himself to man through the *diversities* of nature and cultures, and also that a mature moral sense is adaptable to a multitude of circumstances. Vatican II confirmed this tradition in awesomely pluralistic terms. From a very different direction, Protestant faith has prepared its adherents for eclecticism by affirming subjective confidence in the face of cultural disenchantment. F. D. Maurice and, more recently, H. Richard Niebuhr express this Protestant respect for finite positions by appropriating the principle of John Stuart Mill that men are usually correct in what they affirm and wrong in what they deny. Theologically this principle is interpreted to mean that the Christian can rely on his convictions about Christ and Christianity without confusing his convictions with the absolute Christ or absolute Christianity, and certainly without denying the positive potentialities of opposing convictions.

From another perspective, what we are witnessing in suburban eclecticism is a major move toward the Easternization of Western middle-class society. While expansive man's inability to worry about contradictions in his life-style shocks and disturbs Americans who like neatness both in their kitchens and in their thinking, Orientals may find the expansive life-style as familiar as won ton soup. It is not unusual in Japan, for example, for persons to order various dimensions of their lives within different religious practices and beliefs. The Confucian ethic can easily exist beside Shinto ceremonies and Buddhist concepts of the self. Within Mahayana Buddhism, at a temple center such as Mt. Kenya in Japan, a believer can wander from building to building and confront the eternal Buddha nature in many diverse forms, from the Great Sun Buddha to the Buddha of the Western Paradise, who saves those who faithfully call upon him, to the Goddess of Mercy, the Buddha nature that helps the faithful in their daily tasks. The Buddha nature is manifold. Its perfection resides in its ability to realize cosmic consciousness—the simultaneous enjoyment of all possibilities and wisdom derived from a multiplicity of perspectives.

Anti-Intellectualism

Not only is the expansive radical impatient with his neighbors who try to maintain a neat, consistent style of life, he is also uneasy with so-called intellectuals, even though he may be enrolled in a university or adult education program, and even though others may look upon him as an intellectual. In the academic setting, he is a man without a country. He is frustrated by the cool, abstract approach of his instructors, because this style seems so bloodless. But he tends to produce theories about the irrelevance of theories. In fact, the whole encounter between expansive man and the intellectual takes on the atmosphere of a stagy, mock battle fought over fictional issues. The expansive style seems intent on opposing a curiously stereotyped opponent: intellectualism, made to appear devoid of feeling, impractical, unconcerned, irrelevant.

At points in the mock battle, issues appear that are genuine, although they are not usually the issues that are acknowledged. Predictably, they are issues connected with contrasting styles, akin to the clashes experienced when personalities with conflicting chemistries meet. The expansive style is dabbling, comprehensive, faddish, impatient with discipline and methodology, not concerned about the pride of workmanship. In his own thinking, the suburban radical is far more concerned about whether problems are interesting and relevant. Akin to the spirit of many contemporary artists, his style pays more attention to the process of the task at hand—whether the work is done with spirit, imagination, and passion—than he does to the finished product.

But from the viewpoint of persons who are concerned about carefulness of thought and about mastering a problem, the expansive style appears irresponsible. If the radical's tendency is to dabble in a series of flashy projects, they say he should be branded for what he is: a showman, not a serious thinker. Furthermore, the radical's impatience with persons who recognize the complexity of issues is insulting. He demands from them abridgments, summaries, popularizations, and descriptions of the kernel of issues, while they object that insight requires effort.

Recently, we had occasion to participate in a university's urban semester—a full-time, sixteen-unit course with largely middle- and upper middle-class students and faculty (most of them definitely expansive). During the semester, an unwritten rule developed that, in class conversations, even "mini lectures" were to be avoided, evidently because what needed to be said could be said in brief, pithy remarks. The semester's curriculum was to be a spectrum ranging from impressionistic tours through city streets to visits from technical experts and urban operators. What happened in these visits was predictable: the visitors had difficulty expressing themselves, straining to try to fill in background information, while most of the students had not taken the trouble to prepare themselves. The one methodology section of the course was canceled early in the game. At the end of the semester, however, the embarrassing encounters were forgotten and the course was deemed a success, not because anyone had learned a great deal about any single issue or group of issues, but because the process had been worthwhile. Most of the students and faculty were more concerned about participating in a relevant series of events in which they might discover themselves than in building a stack of information about urban crises.

The expansive man, then, seems preoccupied with the process, whereas the intellectual seems more intent on building a product: a mass of information, insight into truth, mastery of an area, or a marketable skill. The expansive man seems perennially ready to be playful in his thought, whereas the intellectual's playfulness is in tension with his devotion to craftsmanship. The expansive man feels satisfied when he has participated in an alive happening, whereas the intellectual circumscribes his enthusiasm with quasi-moral criteria for evaluating effectiveness.

But the tension is more profound than this, in that the playfulness of the radical disassociates itself from the traditional concerns of the Western intellect—the concern for comprehensiveness and meaning. At least since the sixth century B.C., the Western intellectual has been trying to bring order out of chaos, to find the system of thought that might include all partial truths, to discover first principles, and to make generalizations about the laws that characterize the behavior of man, his thought, and his environment. The expansive man, though, has apparently given up the ghost. He has not repudiated the effort to bring order out of chaos, but he has lost interest in the task. It is a job that used to be done, was never finished, but now does not seem worth the energy. There is more beauty and more excitement in playfully exploring a number of world views, all of which exist side by side as the perspectives of faith. The suburban radical sometimes finds himself wondering what it was that Plato thought was so bad about chaos!

Intellectual playfulness, in open rebellion against reason's seriousness, also casts suburban radicality in a role that is actively subversive—or so it appears to a number of observers. For years, social critics who have written out of an involvement in neo-Freudian theory have demonstrated that playfulness erodes the goal-directed mentality required by capitalism-socialism—a mentality promoted by the Western intellectual establishment. But only recently has Herbert Marcuse argued that intellectual playfulness may now be the sole revolutionary force of any significance in America. In his *Essay on Liberation,* Marcuse describes "the new sensibility," the playful mentality, as a shattering attack on the spirit of the age, far more devastating than the taut violence that substitutes one set of paternalists for another. "The insistence that a socialist society can and ought to be light, pretty, playful, that these qualities are essential elements of freedom, the faith in the rationality of the imagination, the demand for a new morality and culture"—all constitute a rebellion with new agents of radical change.[11] The protest is total, reaching even to the previously apolitical, aesthetic dimension, slashing at the dictates of repressive reason.

Marcuse finds the best example of this rebellion in the hippie subculture's playful use of Establishment words, such as "pot," "grass," "trip," "acid," to refer to objects or activities tabooed by the Establishment. He also sees it in the psychedelic search and in new forms of contemporary art: nonobjective painting and sculpture, stream-of-consciousness and formalistic literature, twelve-tone composition, blues, and jazz. These do more than merely multiply the creative products of the advanced industrial age. "They dissolve the very structure of perception" to make way for a new kind of society.[12]

The revolutionary agents, the playful elite, Marcuse identifies with the New Left, and he finds little or no evidence that suburbia is spawning such an elite. Suburbia is the victim of its conservative, materialist mentality molded by the mass media, which in turn reflect the interest of the military-industrial combine. But here is precisely the point where Marcuse is not accurate. He fails to see that middle-class suburbia is the seedbed out of which playful anti-intellectualism springs. The phenomenon has little to do with the New Left as an isolated revolutionary movement, and almost nothing to do with the generation gap. Hard as it might be for the disillusioned student in the dirty leather jacket to accept, the lady in the fur coat who does her shopping at Saks and who daily proves her anti-intellectuality by blasting the eggheads and by flitting superficially from interest to interest is on his side in the war against reason. She may even be the general, not the private who arrives late on the scene.

Sensuality

The playfulness of expansive man moves easily beyond the realm of ideas, ideologies, and vocabulary to encompass a wide and rich measure of sensual enjoyment. Suburbanites have become absolutely fascinated with the body as a totality—its movement, its contours, its possibilities. Body awareness assumes almost religious proportions, with hoary sandstone churches sponsoring awareness groups for housewives, often in time slots normally reserved for sewing circles and missionary aid societies. A Roman Catholic retreat center periodically sponsors sessions in which a predominantly female clientele will practice "being open" to bodily sensations, will "touch the air," will wave their arms dreamily to experience the grace of being physical, and will spend long moments witnessing the rhythms of breath and heartbeat. Male suburbanites are less drawn to such forms of body awareness, but when associated with more acceptable sensivity training experiences, the men can wig-

gle their seats as well as their lady folk and can thoroughly
enjoy the attempt to communicate in nonverbal ways.

In the process, the radical is discovering the vast difference between sensuality and sexiness. The new suburban
style is most definitely sensuous and affirmative of the
body's integrity, while occasional lapses into sexiness are
regarded as the intrusion of slang into literate dialogue.
Those who have participated in the nude swimming periods at the adult education center at Esalen, for example,
report their amazement with the experience. It is mind-
stretching; it is an encounter with all the superstitions,
fears, and shame connected with the body in our culture; it
is a new possibility for middle-class relatedness (Esalen
courses are not inexpensive); and it is a possibility for a
relaxed naturalness wherein the person's entire sensorium
is actuated and tenderly directed to other *persons*. Rather
than the sharp, specific, and impersonal sex drive, what is
developed and allowed to blossom is a capacity for thor-
oughgoing, personal, and embodied relation. Sensuality can
include sexual expression, but it need not—and the discovery is something of a "Great Awakening" for our times.

Body awareness is also becoming an enormously significant basis for social relatedness on the home front.
Y.M.C.A.'s and Y.W.C.A.'s, of course, have long been
centers of socialization as well as of body-building. But the
last fifteen years have brought an unprecedented expansion
of health club–community centers. The sweaty gymnasium
has virtually disappeared and in its place is an endless variety of commercial clubs devoted to exercise, reducing, and
individual and team sports. Jogging takes place in parks,
where a kind of fraternity grows among the runners. And
reducing enthusiasts are organizing for mutual support.

Body awareness communities are different from those
traditionally produced in suburbia by team sports. Highly
competitive situations are frowned upon in many circles,
and the image of Little League fathers nagging their sons

to higher and finer triumphs now at best seems anachronistic, at worst heretical within the doctrinal orthodoxy of body awareness. Instead, these communities more often draw persons for whom sports have been embarrassing—persons who cannot relax with their own physical awkwardness. They are a fellowship of the halt, the fat, the thin, the lonely, and those for whom suburban ease spells lethargy. The organizing process is one where there is a frank acceptance of disabilities—a process not dissimilar to that of Alcoholics Anonymous—and a kind of humorous, fresh building of fellowship around rituals of physical confession and physical salvation.

This expansion of body awareness, in spite of lapses into a comic narcissism, can be interpreted epochally—the development of what Norman O. Brown, following Freud, calls polymorphous perversity, "delighting in that full life of all the body." [13] The style, he claims, is Dionysian, which is intensely this-worldly and which revels in the profuseness of the sensual. Instead of approaching the physical as an object to be dominated by reason, the Dionysian finds in the physical a vision of cosmic beauty to be revered as having value in itself. The physical, associated in Western culture with repression and guilt, assumes its rightful coequality with other facets of the human situation and becomes both the vehicle for human liberation and the mode of enjoyment associated with that liberation. Brown connects the Dionysian style with what he calls body mysticism, which grows in the West out of the Judeo-Christian tradition as affected by alchemy. He contrasts this Western variety of mysticism, "which stays with life, which is the body, and seeks to transform and perfect it," with Apollonian, or sublimation mysticism. This is the tradition popularly identified with the Oriental flight from the physical world and interpreted for Western minds by Evelyn Underhill and Aldous Huxley.[14]

Brown's distinction here between Dionysian and Apollonian styles vastly oversimplifies the situation for both Eastern and Western mysticism; but more seriously, it hides the degree to which suburban sensuality must be viewed as another step in the Easternization of the American middle class. Observers of the suburban scene have noted that persons who are attracted to Eastern mysticism are often deeply involved in suburbia's body awareness groups—a fact that is baffling if Oriental styles encourage a depreciation of the physical. In fact, Eastern mysticism is as many-faceted as its Western analogue, and Westerners can find there an affirmation of body-soul unity that appears in stark contrast to the dualism of body and soul that has come to characterize the doctrines of popular Christian piety. The bodily disciplines of Yoga and the rites of Tantric Buddhism, directed toward identification with the "cosmic body," argue not so much for flight from the sensuous as for an experience of the indivisibility of body and soul in man's quest for the ultimate. The Oriental religious mentality may attempt to earn a final escape from the wheel of life, but this attempt is not a narrowly spiritualized affair. Oriental mysticism, like Dionysian mysticism, resists dualisms and oppositions in the human estate and develops a doctrine of creation that finds in nature a richness to be enjoyed in its own terms. If anything, Apollonian mysticism breaks the bonds of rationalism and plunges the questing individual into a therapeutic process where the redemptive experience is one of wholeness.

If expansive openness to the sensual can be tied to a suburban assimilation of Eastern styles, it can also be represented as a rediscovery of foundational themes within the Judeo-Christian tradition, particularly its doctrine of the created universe. At the heart of the Judeo-Christian faith is precisely the rejection of hostility to the human body and to the physical universe—an affirmation that the body is to be enjoyed because it is a witness to God's persistent creative presence. The Judeo-Christian views have been affected by memories of the Fall, wherein all of nature is seen to have been alienated from the Creator. But the hope is not for an escape from the fallen order. It is for redemption, in which "the trees shall clap their hands," and in which the body will be enjoyed in all its resurrected splendor.

Our conviction is that this distinctively Western celebration of physical realities is undergoing a kind of reinvigoration in expansive locales and that it is making possible a fresh materialism of great ethical consequence. "Personalist" materialism, we might call it: the declaration in Martin Buber's *I and Thou,* so often overlooked in our excitement over his descriptions of interpersonal relationships, that man's true life is not only in relation and meeting with fellowmen but also in meeting with animals and things! Real meeting with nonhuman creatures is possible when we bring them into the circle of personhood; when we treat them with a (nonclinical) respect for their wholeness and autonomy. This is not mysticism or panpsychism; it springs from deep Biblical, personalist wells. For reasons not entirely apparent to us, expansive man seems to be open to this Buberian doctrine. He seems to be engaged in materialism that assigns some space for nonhuman creatures in the realm of ends rather than tools. It is as if he were dipping down into his past and renewing those early childhood days, when, as Ernst Cassirer has pointed out in his studies of language, he spoke to things, toys, chairs, because the paradigm of relationship for children is always personal, always social.

Nostalgia

Because the suburban radical does not totally identify with any one community, cause, or commitment, he deprives himself of that sense of history in which Western man has traditionally reveled. The sense of history is sharpest when a person is able to remember a past in which he and his people have come into being and in which they have achieved their common identity. Thus, the Jewish community ritually remembers the adventures of Abraham, Isaac, and Moses, not just because they were the founding fathers, but because their very memory constitutes a way of saying who and what the Jewish people are. They are the heirs of Abraham, Isaac, and Moses, who in the desert forged a covenant with God. The Jews are the chosen people, who forever must measure the success of their common life in terms of their faithfulness to the social contract made on Mt. Sinai by Moses. Likewise, the Daughters of the American Revolution would have no identity apart from their stories of the revolutionary fathers. And the Democratic Party would be impoverished without its mythologized memories of Jefferson, Jackson, Wilson, Franklin Roosevelt, and John Kennedy.

But who are the fathers of the suburban radical—detached and playful as he is with belief systems and communal loyalties? How does he extend his story into the past? What is his experience of history? In almost a cartooned fashion, expansive man's more expansive children are demonstrating possible answers. Off at the ivy halls, many of the middle-class students have taken that last, dreadful step of alienation from the mythologies of their national and religious past and, for all intents and purposes, consider themselves to be starting afresh, without precedent. They see themselves as barbarians crossing the mountains to do something new within a culture grown jaded. They do not look to their communities' pasts for inspiring tales of moral heroism or for the vision of a viable mission. When moral heroes are found, they usually are surprisingly contemporary, co-participators in a new communal cause—the Revolution, perhaps. Thus, pictures of Mao may adorn their dormitory windows.

But the history-deprived students have developed a buoyant ability to deal with the past playfully. For example, a tour of clothing stores frequented by expansive youth will show a collection of styles and fads from periods and places throughout man's history. In fashion, we are accustomed to commenting on the fact that styles have a way of repeating themselves ("Save your mother's party dress because it will be high fashion in thirty years, give or take a few tactical stitches here and there"). The fashions of expansive youth, however, are something again. They include Martha Washington ruffles, flapper dresses, Edwardian suits, Abe Lincoln topcoats, peasant skirts, Colombian sport shirts, uniforms from past wars, Indian beads, Davy Crockett hats, pioneer dresses, Tundra furs, and on and on. The fashionable clothing stores are like a giant chain of attics, where slightly aged Bobbsey Twins can play dress-up with Granny's clothes, and the overall effect is one of a completely enjoyable historical game. Expansive man's offspring and the industries that serve his whims seem to be cultivating an appreciative immersion in the textures and styles of the past without the concomitant loyalties to identity-giving traditions. The past is not so much the memory of our collective childhood as it is a manufactured potpourri. Expansive youth have many pasts, and they can take these off and put them on as easily as a Napoleonic uniform. They are incurably nostalgic, and their experience of history can best be described as nostalgic.

We recently met an affluent suburban dentist who embodies this nostalgic spirit in a remarkable way. He confides that he recently has furnished a second office, more for his own enjoyment than for the treatment of patients. In fact, he rarely sees patients there. The furnishings are Early American; the wallpaper is red velvet; and the dental equipment is largely antique. There he can be at peace with himself, enjoying an atmosphere that is both simpler and more sensuous than that of his stainless steel, pastel-lighted office.

The vision of the dentist reminiscing amid the best past that his money could buy borders on the comic, but his style is widely dispersed among suburban radicals. The expansive style deals with the past very respectfully and loves to become involved thoroughly in the details of antique cars, guns, cut glass, pottery, artifacts, and period furniture. The stance, however, is detached, and the value of the past is either in its sensual enjoyment or in its ability to evoke nostalgic feelings. To be sure, having the past around on shelves and in garages is a mark of status, revealing that the suburbanite has the time and money to follow through on such an exhausting process of collection. Yet the grasping for status does not exhaustively account for what is going on. Mainly, the suburban radical is working out a way of handling the past—presumably a human necessity—that is consistent with his eclectic intellectual habits and with his high valuation on experience.

One who is playful with community loyalties needs a way of being playful with the past; these are complementary elements of the same phenomenon. In nostalgic experiences, radicals can acknowledge that they are heirs of the past, but they can do so without relinquishing their own sovereignty. Nostalgia can be turned on and off; nostalgia-producing objects can be placed on the proper shelves, thereby limiting experiences of the past to the desired time and place. The expansive man thus asserts his freedom through maintaining control over his own past.

This control is possible, especially because so many of the occasions for nostalgia cost money. Purchasing an object or buying a ticket becomes the gate through which the affluent individual usually has to pass to claim an opportunity for exercising his nostalgia. It takes considerable money, for example, to buy an early American history for the home in the shape of Currier and Ives prints, wallpaper, and maple end tables, particularly if the suburbanite is a hard rock and can be stimulated only by "authentic" antiques. And it takes considerable money and effort to buy and read biographies, memoirs, and histories, which currently provide a focus of the nostalgia market, particularly among relatively well educated expansive men.

The life-story market deserves additional comment because it is part of a larger nostalgic happening in the suburbs—a flourishing curiosity about the poetry of human personalities. The life stories currently being sold are not of the variety that concentrates on mechanical chronological accounts. The fashion centers on books such as Carl Sandburg's biography of Lincoln and on other historical-artistic attempts to portray the poetry of life-styles. What expansive man wants from other people approaches a mystical experience of union, and it is certainly more an aesthetic demand than a rational one. The same desire to explore aesthetically the lives of others, to be nostalgic about the past of others, can be seen in the enlarged importance assigned to birthdays by expansive men. A revolt against impersonal birthday celebrations (cake, "Happy Birthday to You," presents) is under way, and the suburbs are beginning to hatch some new celebrative forms. We are aware, for example, of several families who visit each other on birthdays simply to encourage the celebrant to reminisce about his own past and to speak about what things are important to him. Another family invites to its home on birthdays the persons who have provided the most beautiful presence in the celebrant's life during the past year, and the party is spent nostalgically indulging in mutual memories of the year.

The nostalgic style is extremely subtle and difficult to maintain without lapsing into the maudlin heresy. To be maudlin is to take an emotional bath with the water turned up high, whereas to be nostalgic about the past is to re-create its moods and emotions in a wishful, but nevertheless detached, manner. The nostalgic experience of history is always at the edge of idealizing the past, seeing it as better than the present, because the nostalgic memory is carefully edited and drawn in pleasing strokes. But the nostalgic past does not serve moral purposes, as do the crisp pictures of golden ages drawn by Western philosophers. It does not steel the will to reform the present. Instead, its contribution is more gamelike, its function more calculated to enliven the present by filling it with the richness of nostalgic emotions, which become aesthetic ends in themselves.

The nostalgically remembered past—even in its comic dimensions—should not be put down as a loss of the sense of history. The expansive style masquerades as ahistorical, concerned only with fulfillment of present potentialities, and concentrated on denying the past an authoritative role. Fashions, costumes, party decorations, phonograph records, and home furnishings hardly seem to be the stuff through which the grandeur of human history is best preserved. Yet nostalgia functions responsibly in relation to the serious sense of history and is a form of community memory whose integrity deserves discovery and affirmation.

Nostalgia functions in relation to history in a way that is analogous to the medieval court jester's mocking of the king. The jester makes the king laugh, and he alone is able to bare the pretenses of court pomposity. But the deformed, demented clown is welcomed into the courtly circle because his presence is needed. He saves the king from the pitfall of being overly impressed with his own power and provides a humorous occasion for self-transcendence. When the jester dances, the king sees himself as a dancing fool; he is more capable of dealing with his own humanity.

Nostalgia is the sense of history that belongs to man as the "laughing animal" and as the animal who needs to be reminded of his own estate. Nostalgia needs to be in close relation to the ritualistic recitals of community memories in public ceremonies and to the academic exploration of history, simply because nostalgia provides perspective and comic relief. It may even be the way that attention to the past is preserved, as, for example, when the alienated youth

rejects "the American ideology" but maintains his cultural identity through wearing red, white, and blue patches
on his trousers. Likewise, suburbia is crowded with Jews
who have relaxed their identification with the memory
of Moses, but who nevertheless hold on to their Jewish past
nostalgically. Nostalgia has an emotive power that contributes to, and does not destroy, the other more elevated
functions of the historical consciousness.

Stylistic Community

Memories of the past have traditionally functioned to
give individuals and groups a sense of identity that extends
beyond the life-span of individuals. The past has provided
the cement for joining persons into communities. But for
expansive man, history ceases to serve this function and
nostalgic emotions become one kind of workable substitute. Communities may be made up of persons who are
able to be nostalgic together, even though they may not be
nostalgic about similar pasts. It is enough that persons be
able to affirm their own pasts in romanticized fashion and
that they be able to do so in ways that can be relived and
appreciated by others.

The shared nostalgic mood illustrates what must be
called a radical shift in the American experience of community. The shift is from content to stylistic community,
which involves a transition in the forms of dogmatism that
characterize expansive suburbia. Among expansive persons, community is not threatened by the sharpest disagreements about politics or social policy. But what does
threaten it is the presence of persons who cannot play the
sharply defined life game with zest; persons who, for example, cannot abide the corny enjoyment that goes along
with Abe Lincoln topcoats and Dr. Zhivago hats, and who
have a way of letting the steam out of an otherwise en-

chanted moment. Style can maintain its social power only when everyone is willing to play, since those who are caught in their playful romps by unsympathetic persons will inevitably feel a little embarrassed and childish. Unsympathetic persons have to be eliminated.

The notion that the new character ideal is anticommunity, as argued by Philip Rieff, is erroneous. The coming of expansive man to the suburb does not spell the end of suburban institutions, but may signal a change in that which holds them together. If anything, expansive man is more clannish than his forefathers, yet institutions that think they can keep his loyalty out of an allegiance to belief systems will think that expansive man is anarchic. Churches, for example, will have to face declining memberships as long as they rest their case solely on doctrines. But they can expect a renaissance when they learn the invigorating power of style—when they discover that alive communities are increasingly bound together for stylistic reasons. The expansive gospel of nostalgia, for example, may seem pale beside the doctrine of justification by faith, but the two are not incompatible. And ultimately, the expansive experience of community may prove to be a saving presence for the ancient institutions of the West, now so threatened.

Chapter 3

THE GENESIS
OF EXPANSIVE MAN

BUT WHY should the American suburb prove to be such hospitable territory for expansive man? What is it that turns conscientious suburban gentlemen into cultural radicals? The suburban atmosphere allows for the appearance of incredibly malleable imaginations. The predisposition for any radical character change is the possession of a flexible image-making organ. Character is largely a matter of self-picturing, and character change assumes the ability to make new pictures. In the case of the current transition into expansiveness, wherein change itself becomes a norm, we can assume that the image-making organ, the imagination, is going practically all the time, making fundamentally new images for and of the self and society. The suburb does not encourage the production of totalitarian images, the kind that might captivate and perhaps shut down the imagination. But the suburb does encourage imagination and its free play; that is what suburban education and entertainment are all about. So it is not surprising that suburbanites are capable of radical shifts in self-imagery.

But why now, at this late date, do suburbanites shift into the expansive self-image? One answer could suffice. The American middle class is perennially ripe for movements that emphasize the passions as against the intellect, the practical as against the reflective, the natural as against the artificial, the intuitive as against the reasonable. The suburb, even at this point in the twentieth century, is not very far from the pioneer forefathers who rejected European civilization for the expansiveness of nature and for the instability of frontier energies. In spite of the technical sophistication required by post-Sputnik enterprise, the middle class, as always, seems committed to the remarkable task of building a culture that will show how much can be done without scholarly pretensions.

The situation is, and always has been, extremely volatile. It could and did erupt into the spectacular back-to-God movement of the fifties, just as in the nineteenth century it supported the series of Great Revivals. It could and did panic into a poisonous crusade against Marxist and liberal equivalents of the witches of Salem. It could and did respond to university crises of the 1960's by withdrawing funds and forcing a destructive withdrawal of political support from public higher education in spite of the economic advantages of this system. In short, the eternal irrationalism of the American middle class provides ripe ground for the emergence of a characterological ideal that is more consistent with frontier pragmatism and energism than with the American ideologies that were born in the living rooms of Enlightenment philosophers.

The Scientific Spirit as Expansive Mentality

We would not have predicted a few years ago, though, that the middle class would maintain its irrational lifestyles, and we certainly would not have imagined that these could blossom into the ebullient expansive ideal. In fact, in the 1950's all the evidence seemed to the contrary. The suburbs were being populated by gray-flanneled executives, engineers, practical scientists, mathematicians, and tech-

nicians; and their behavior did not create much confidence
that the precious suburban setting would be transformed
into a swinging scene. If anything, we would have guessed
that technocracy was finally here—that suburbia would be
drab but efficient, that the fun of the Brave New World
might increasingly hold attraction as an escape from the
intolerably boorish engineering mentality of the middle
class.

But we were wrong, and our failure was partly in our inability to grasp the expansive potential of the scientific
spirit that is idealized by suburbanites. Actually, it is a very
short step from the empirical notion that truth is what is
verifiable by experience to the expansive belief that experience itself is valuable—that it may even be the highest
good. From there it is but another short step to the notion
that the richest life is the one that includes the most varied
kinds of experiences. The style of the suburban radical is
not as it appears—a backlash against the stainless-steel
grayness of a scientific atmosphere—but instead is the predictable spin-off from a culture that is infatuated with scientific experimentalism.

If, as has been observed again and again, the scientific
age has made it more difficult to affirm eternal truths in a
confident manner, one can expect persons to turn to their
own experience as a court of final appeal. Middle-class
radicals, both adults and youth, who currently are testing
experiential possibilities in order to avoid the devastating
superficiality of a culture shaped by the practical sciences,
are doing so as children of the very sciences they seek to
avoid. Forced to appeal to their experience, they are finding in experience a cause for celebration. But they are
tempted to ignore the fact that their pagan joys are so
closely joined to their empirical achievements.

We also did not understand that the scientific spirit had
a way of exploding into the most blatant kind of playfulness with perspectives—a way of fooling around with dif-

ferent modes of handling data. We laymen had accepted
the myth that science is objective. But our scientific neighbors, particularly the more intelligent ones, were not so
deceived, and they could easily agree with Bertrand Russell's warning against the doctrine of immaculate perception. We should have had more sense. Even as early as the
eighteenth century, the somewhat ill-starred philosopher
Johann Fichte had dared to suggest that the world is a very
different place for different individuals, depending on the
point of view that individuals assume. Individuals and societies, he argued, create the worlds where they choose to
live, and their creative possibility is the mark of their freedom.

In our own era, Fichte's insight has been remarkably
confirmed by developments in quantum physics, which in-
sists that our understanding of the structure of nature is
conditioned by the limitations of our perspective. And the
spirit of quantum physics is mirrored in the mathematical
practices out of which the miracles of suburban engineering are produced. Prospective engineers, practical scientists, and suburban schoolchildren who master the obscuri-
ties of the new math know that there is nothing sacred
about any particular mathematical system. What you do in
math depends on your perspective—the assumptions and
definitions with which you start. Playfulness is the name of
the game. Although the scientific spirit has its serious side,
scholars and practitioners are more attracted to the scientific disciplines for the fun they afford—the ability to play
with different perspectives, to see how things look if one
adopts alternative assumptions. Little wonder that the expansive life-style should flower in suburbia, where the scientific mentality thrives. Had the expansive style not emerged,
sooner or later the women and children would have accused
the science-minded fathers of keeping all the fun for themselves.

Not so obvious is the fact that the scientific spirit has

often had a way of generating mystical sensitivities—intuitions of the grandeur, mystery, organic unity, sensual depth, and utter beauty of the universe and of man's nature. Einstein, for example, argued that science is founded upon and inseparable from such a vision. And Aldous Huxley sought in the mystical experience of the peyote drug cult the culmination of his scientific pursuits. The scientist-philosopher Michael Polanyi could not conceive of scientific procedures apart from insight into nature's wholeness and apart from a solid trust in the intuitive faculties that afford this insight. In Christian theology, it was the paleontologist Teilhard de Chardin who tore the veil that concealed man's infinite possibility and the universe's mysterious life energies. He invited pragmatic, scientific men to go with him on a mystical adventure, and his point was that scientific men are not fully aware of their world unless they can revel in its grandeur. In this same spirit, the physicist Ouspensky has become the pied piper for the current student generation, ushering them into a mystical realm that reveals both the height and depth of human sensuality and spiritual reality.

So the science-minded suburb stands ready, and perhaps even has a propensity, for mystical revival. This propensity was only obscured by the frenetic preoccupation with achieving national engineering excellence in the late 1950's and 1960's, but even this preoccupation made the revival more inevitable. The pressures were building up because persons were not finding a way to legitimate the mystical experience, the natural culmination of their scientific mentality. The suburbs were indeed prepared for a new, radical character ideal that could provide such a legitimation. In an important sense, the logic of scientific experimentalism, its tendency to demand an intuition of nature's wholeness, became the vehicle by which closely guarded Western doors were opened to the profuse religious experience of the Orient.

The Expansive Response to Social Change

That the scientific spirit should serve as a precondition of cultural radicality is really not so surprising, particularly in the light of an important catalytic agent: the fact of unrestrained, undirected, and constantly accelerating social change in the Western world. Nurtured by the pure and practical sciences, valuable resources are habitually channeled into innovation, with the predictable consequence that change becomes accepted as an unquestioned way of life—a new situation for Western man. In this situation, beliefs take on a faddish character and the convictions of today are qualified by the gnawing awareness that they might well be archaic tomorrow.

In fact, it is assumed that beliefs, like everything else, cannot remain static—that they ought to reflect the total culture's commitment to flux. Supposedly "eternal" philosophies are placed in almost the same category as "camp" art objects such as Coca-Cola lampshades or Gainsborough's painting of *Pinky*.

In the face of permanent flux, suburbia is responding by cultivating a privatistic life-style, calculated to provide security in one's own private experience. The suburbanite initiates a radical search for interesting, provocative experiences, a process that is not threatened by the fact that individuals do not seem to control in significant ways the directions of massive cultural transformation. The search is by and large carried on alone, or it is limited to small cliques of friends or family groups which, without much effort, serve as comfortable extensions of individual identity. Indeed, as Kenneth Keniston points out, the bravado extroversion of Teddy Roosevelt, who sought heightened experience in heroic behavior and public acclaim, seems comic in the present setting.

Within the privatistic quest for experience, issues re-

lated to political-social change may even be transformed
into subjective experiential terms; and simple ways of operating in the face of confusing flux can thus be found. In
the 1960's, for example, the civil rights movement achieved
a remarkable momentum in America—a momentum that
was carried into a radical student politics, which in turn
accelerated the polarization of suburban politics. At the
same time, cities were entering an alarming period of turmoil, and it was becoming clear that to do nothing was
simply to heighten the process of decay. In brief, it was a
decade of enormous change, and expedient political solutions to urban problems were desperately needed. The privatistic suburban bias, however, tended to discourage interest in questions of expedient politics and sought to
translate urban issues into subjective problems of human
relations. The suburbs literally blossomed with sensitivity
groups; and churches filled their calendars with interracial
encounters.

From one perspective, then, the suburbs reacted to the
turbulence of the 1960's with the old conservative waiting
game: the idea that society would be reformed only as
people are transformed or as people get to know each other
(thereby ignoring urgent social policy needs). But from
another perspective, the suburban response was expansive.
It subsumed political matters within its private quest for
experience and made baffling social change into the occasion for organizing interesting, emotion-rending, shocking
events. Tragically, instead of pondering together the intri-
cate injustices of the city, state, and national taxation systems, suburbanites swapped tales about how they really
got to the nitty-gritty in an interracial encounter, how they
were shocked when the Black Power advocate "told it like
it was," how saddened they were about conditions in a
neighborhood service center, or how they were working
out forms of honest social relatedness in a sensitivity group.

Expansive privatism finds a more extreme and potentially more dangerous expression in suburbia's dabbling with mystical experiences. Here the radical suburbanite finds that he can deal with heightened social change by denying its reality. The mystical experience, whether created by means of drugs or by the disciplines of Eastern religion, ushers its devotees into a changeless realm and generates both a sense of immortality and a feeling of metaphysical unity with fellowmen and with nature. The adventure, however, is wrongly interpreted as a cheap escape from the ills of social change. It can be represented as a head-on approach to the most basic problems of human alienation. But a danger is omnipresent—the possibility that mystical mind expansion can too easily become a privatistic form of dropping out, and can end in a gushy self-indulgence that refuses to see that flux creates social hells as well as the stimulus for leisurely mystical experimentalism.

Another extreme expression of the privatistic response to social change is playfulness with religious, philosophical, and moral beliefs. Kenneth Keniston, in his study of social change and American youth, observes that social change promotes a detachment from deep commitments and a peculiarly eighteenth-century aversion to enthusiasms of all kinds.[15] What Keniston finds among youth is, of course, not difficult to find in their mothers and fathers, who are equally overwhelmed by social change. But Keniston wrongly concludes that this detachment inevitably issues in a disinterested neglect of commitment systems. It can also transform these commitment systems ("modes of experiencing the world") into playthings. The evidence that supposedly ultimate positions are not so ultimate can free persons to enjoy their commitment systems while not being burdened with feelings of hypocrisy for failing to live consistently within them. Social flux can free the radical to play with experiencing the world as a Christian *and* a Buddhist, a humanist *and* a mystic, a scientist *and* an astrologer. He does not experience his eclecticism as an absence of seriousness, but rather as a serious use of freedom to enrich his experience. He can react to social flux by incorporating its various styles into his own life pattern, and he can maintain both the new and the old without their engaging in a personality warfare of mutual destruction.

Pluralism and Expansiveness

Playfulness is more directly related, however, to the suburb's relatively new experience with pluralism. Suburbanites today are feeling pluralism in a sharp manner, and may even be the first American generation to be forced into an adjustment to pluralistic facts of life. Admittedly, America has for at least a century been the homeland for Protestants, Jews, and Catholics, and it has played host to Buddhist temples, Vedanta societies, and Islamic mosques, as well as to a vast number of small sectarian groups. It has maintained several languages; and in spite of the perpetual state of economic and political tension, it has managed to keep a number of races from open warfare. Still, in its political and social life, America until recently proceeded as a Protestant nation. Culturally, we were descendants of Martin Luther and John Calvin. When social critics referred to America's Protestant ethic, it was as likely to be observed dutifully by the Beverly Hills Jew as by the New England Congregationalist. We all attended the Christmas pageant at the local high school, went caroling down Christmas-tree lane, and celebrated the Easter holidays.

But in the 1950's something happened. Jews boycotted Christmas pageants—or, more threatening to the Protestant ethos, they demanded equal time. Prayers were removed from the public schools in deference to the sensitivities of a group whose existence had hardly been acknowledged: the atheists. By the 1960's, America's pluralistic elasticity was further tested by a Roman Catholic

President and the birth of civil rights, protest, and radical groups, both on the right and the left. What had once been a theory about pluralistic society, bound to beliefs about free speech and freedom of conscience, became an experience of testing, and the extreme relativity of American ideologies was felt widely for the first time—at least by the majority of Christians. It was felt especially by the Protestants, because, of course, the Protestant monopoly on cultural ritual was under attack.

The period of pluralistic sensitization was also the period in which suburbanites were being bombarded with images of other cultures. The expanding TV market added the dimension of sight to the cosmopolitan education that radio had given to middle-class homes. In addition, the movie industry moved out of the Hollywood sound stages and made familiarity with foreign countrysides into one of the little luxuries that the suburban family could easily provide for its children (and on birthdays, for the whole neighborhood gang). Not only did television and the movies provide stark evidence that all the world was not like the suburb and that not all the world had been baptized in the name of the Father, Son, and Holy Spirit, it provided this evidence in a unique style—superficially, in flashes, in mini dramas, in half-hour blocks, like a kaleidoscope where the pieces will not stay in place long enough to be thoroughly absorbed or appreciated. The style was not judgmental. It did not present its material in such a way that suburbanites had to choose among the array of life possibilities. The media were playful and commercial.

Very few could avoid the message here: that human culture is a highly variable phenomenon, that beliefs appear to be relative to time and place, and that one may not have to make serious judgments about the validity of cultural alternatives. Logically, of course, the fact of cultural relativity does not have to lead to the conclusion that all belief systems are equally valid. It is entirely possible that whole cultures can be morally sick or morally progressive. But in the light of suburban exposure to the mass media, it was difficult to feel an impulse to cross-cultural criticism. Far more in keeping with the spirit of the media was the propensity to enjoy the perspectives of different cultures, or different points of view, seeing that each held the possibility of enrichment or impoverishment. Dogmatism seemed anachronistic. Play seemed sophisticated.

Affluence and Expansiveness

The playful style is enabled, sustained, and repeatedly energized by the affluence of suburban America. We are not arguing, of course, that the middle class has all the money it wants and that it is able to play the field of entertainment possibilities with abandon. If anything, the typical middle-class family hardly knows how to get through the month, and has an extremely difficult time trying to save for the children's education. Affluence, though, is a state of mind. It has to do with relaxation from primal economic fears and with the belief that a number of satisfying options are financially possible. The middle-class family, for example, may not own a mountain cabin, but it can choose to camp, to swim at the beach or lake, or to sit at the neighborhood movie theater. The middle-class youth may choose to drop out and assume an impoverished style of living, but the mark of his affluence is his ability to drop back in at will.

In the suburb, the most economically secure class has traditionally been the adolescent population, and one can easily observe here the close coincidence between the expansive style and affluence. The adolescent in our culture has been an aristocrat, a gentleman of leisure, who does not have to work for an extended period, and who may legitimately play, explore limits, and test the satisfaction of various adult roles. Although his younger brothers and sisters are aristocrats, also, he is old enough to imagine life possibilities that might not occur to them. As Ruth Benedict observes, it is virtually expected that the adolescent will be irresponsible, according to adult standards; [16] Erik Erikson agrees, and describes adolescence as a psychosocial moratorium, set aside for the purpose of experimenting with possible identities.[17]

The affluence of suburbia enables persons to perpetuate the adolescent experience even into adulthood. Affluence makes aristocrats of us all and allows us to enjoy modes of freedom normally reserved for high school or college, precisely because adolescent behavior has less to do with age than with financial security. The joy, abandonment, and ease associated with adolescence, particularly in the gamelike associations of the peer group—the gang—are translated into terms of adult play. Adult symbols and adult manners alter the ethos considerably, but the adolescent reality cannot be concealed for long. And we cannot ignore indefinitely the fact that expansive suburbia is involved in a rousing, mildly hell-raising adolescent renaissance. The styles of puberty are becoming character ideals; and the ideals are experienced as liberation. That the expansive style, supported by affluence, appears as irresponsibility grows from our habit of anger with adolescent fickleness. The perspective that provokes our irritation, though, is changing, and we will have to find alternative ways of keeping young people in their place. The yodel-voiced teen-ager will simply have to pioneer new styles if he is anxious to maintain the disappearing fiction of the generation gap.

The political theorist Herbert Marcuse is highly ambivalent in his attitudes toward the emergence of this affluence-produced elite in American society.[18] On the one hand, he correctly believes that any major cultural transformation must rest on an economic basis—an elimination of the preoccupation with physical survival. He finds in the reduced workweek, in the possibility of a guaranteed annual income, and in the impetus toward reform of archaic welfare systems the promise of new possibilities to pursue distinctively human ends.

On the other hand, Marcuse finds the economic presuppositions of the expansive style to be demonic, because he observes that the success of the industry-advertising sector of the American economy depends on its ability to deprive persons of their freedom. Citizens of the advanced industrial economy are convinced, by means of sophisticated advertising artistry, that they need the objects and services which the economy provides. They believe, Marcuse argues, that they are unfulfilled unless surrounded by capitalistic gadgetry; and they are led, in spite of themselves, to believe that their highest good resides in making the economic superstructure both efficient and smoothly operating. Persons begin to feel, for example, that their vocation is the same as their economic task, and they actually become—as an essential definition of their personhood—bricklayers and lawyers. The vocational choices that persons perceive to be open to them are those that are needed by the economy. Thus, Marcuse's point is that playful, expansive man is deceived. What appears to be his liberation is his enslavement because he has not determined his life-style on the basis of his real needs or his real desires. His needs and desires are artificial—shaped as he receives the cajoling, persuading messages of the nation's advertising industry. Playful man is not a free man, his play being determined by others who have access to the mind-shaping capacities of the mass media.

Marcuse's diagnosis of the institutional, affluent origins of the expansive style is quite disturbing. His analysis cannot be faulted, at least as a broad, prophetic judgment devoid of the niceties of scholarly qualification. The objects and experiences of the expansive style are indeed often manufactured and marketed. Even television's invitation to savor foreign cultures is a commercial product, carefully tailored not to offend or to affect the sponsor's economic interests. But Marcuse's judgments are based on a distinction that must seriously be questioned. The distinction is between real and artificial needs, real and perceived freedom. Persons in the advanced industrial economy perceive themselves as free, and perceive their need for expansion as real. But appearances, he says, are deceptive. The forces of persuasion are beyond man's ability to control because they are not recognized as weapons demonically committed to the manipulation of persons. In fact, the whole structure of needs and desires is artificially produced, oblivious to possibilities for developing a genuinely humane culture. Human potentialities are ignored.

Marcuse's distinction between the real and the perceived renders useful service for his analysis, but it breaks down in the face of close scrutiny, particularly in the effort to describe what real freedom and the satisfaction of real needs would be like. Marcuse rests his case on a forcedly idealistic model of man—a vision of true humanity. Real needs are those necessary to fulfill this ideal; and artificial needs are those projected by the advertising industry but which are not in harmony with true humanity. The position is more Platonic than Marxist.

And it is just this ideal of man that the expansive suburbanite cannot abide. The model seems much too dogmatic, and the subtle task of distinguishing between real and perceived needs, or between real and perceived desires, seems out of touch with the more modest aspirations of the expansive style. Furthermore, the value judgments seem to be misguided. The playfulness of expansive man within his suburban jungle gym—constructed and sold by the industry-advertising complex—appears to be freedom enough because it is so fascinating, satisfying, and enriching. To aspire to some higher ideal is to aspire to be more, or less, than man. It is to reach for an elusive goal that is unrelated to the world as we have known it, and to miss what the world, with all its imperfections, has to offer in the development of a humane existence. Marcuse is just too tense to make good company. He is not even threatening. For expansive man, he simply is a bore.

Even if Marcuse's distinction between artificial and real were to be accepted, a strong case could be made that there is a real need in affluent suburbia for intensive, expanded (even artificial) experience. Carl Fabor, a clinical psychologist at U.C.L.A., speaks about the "Orange County syndrome" when referring to the emotional impoverishment of suburbia at its worst. He argues that suburbanites are robbed of the opportunity to experience savage emotions: fear, covetousness, hunger, hate. They look to retirement years with the security of guaranteed inheritances, delayed income plans, and retirement programs; and the memory of depression years, while sometimes vivid, is nevertheless remote. The youth are deprived even of the opportunity to hate the Russians, in the light of the fact that America has apparently passed beyond the cold war era. In these circumstances, there is a real need to manufacture situations productive of intense feelings. As Fabor suggests, even a bad trip may be better than no trip at all. Suburbia needs to go into the experience market. It needs the colored, flashing lights, the loud high-fidelity music, the restaurants with garish atmospheres, the happenings, and the fads, because without them suburbia would have to find other ways to manufacture a satisfying range of emotions.

The conclusion is startling. Playfulness is enabled not only by affluence. The affluent mentality needs its sights, sounds, feels, and smells in order to maintain its health. The radical mentality of expansive man is not simply a prize the suburbanite seeks in his upward climb. Radicality is the therapy he needs when he arrives.

Chapter 4

NEIGHBORS:
SAVAGE SUBURBANITES

ANYONE who has lived very long within the suburbs knows that communication among neighbors is often a Herculean task. Ideological and temperamental differences, compounded by the normal defensiveness about children's behavior and by the isolated, busy habits of most families, often turn property lines into Berlin walls. If parents can find one or two compatible families on the block (to collect the mail and to pick up newspapers during vacations, to help during emergencies, and to visit), they feel lucky. And, in fact, they feel burdened if neighborhood obligations flourish and become too time-consuming.

Harvey Cox's argument that urban man is liberated, partly because he does not have to like his neighbors or believe that he should cultivate "I–Thou" relationships merely because persons happen to live on the same block, is refreshing. He urges the development of "I–You" relationships, which would include all those public contacts which we do not want to become private.[19] The idea that suburban man should know and love all his neighbors is a holdover from a pre-urban era when persons were not free to select primary relationships from all parts of a geographical area. The liberated suburbanite now roams the metropolitan countryside developing his deepest friendships with little reference to geography, and he usually feels closer to persons who live on the other side of the county than he does to the irritating clan that lives next door.

But expansive man's neighborhood problem is more complex than Cox suggests. It is not a picky, everyday problem of arbitrating conflict or of keeping in or out of the neighbors' hair. It has to do with the conflict of styles and the fact that expansive man's style apparently has the potentiality of drawing fierce backlash movements with important social and political consequences. Further, social interaction in suburbia has an emotional impact on the cultural radical. He sees much of himself in the life-styles of his neighbors, and he is even attracted to them. But he can "see through" his neighbors, and he can never return to the character patterns that they embody. He is like the farm boy who goes to Harvard. He still reads the poetry of Robert Frost, yet now he finds all sorts of philosophical nuances there and he can never again find in Frost the naïve enjoyment he once knew.

The radical's neighborhood problems are further compounded by the instability of the character styles he finds in the suburbs. The suburb is not like a novel by Jean-Paul Sartre, where stereotyped characters play their roles unchangeably, eternally. When we speak of suburban styles, it is an extremely dangerous procedure to pin labels on different individuals and then to expect them to interact according to the script.

In other words, this and the next chapter do not intend to set forth a cast of characters for the suburban drama. They intend, rather, to develop some "ideal types," some models, whose value rests in their ability to help us see the styles of life that interact and conflict within the middle class. The models ought to be an aid in understanding real, concrete suburbanites, yet they are character styles, not necessarily parts of the population. This point must be recognized clearly, because otherwise the models will be utilized in an artificial or an unfair manner.

The mix of suburban styles can be irritating, explosive, fluid, interesting, and unstable. It is like a game more appropriate to Alice in Wonderland than to the Little League field. Different players in the suburb appear to be playing different games. Worse yet, some seem to be playing according to a number of sets of rules, while others change rules in the middle of a play. The suburbanite takes the kickoff, immediately throws the ball through the hoop, and claims a home run!

We do not want to overemphasize instability, however. Suburban styles have a kind of internal strength growing from the fact that various styles provide relatively satisfactory and fulfilling life experiences. There is even an order to suburban characterological change—a predictable progress of social character development. Seasoned observers of the middle class soon learn that the appearance of directionless flux is deceptive—that certain constancies and a certain logic temper the intensity of suburban change.

Søren Kierkegaard, the nineteenth-century philosopher and theologian, probably best describes our underlying notion of life-styles, their transformation, and the relation that they have to one another. In one sense, he argues, life-styles are rival views of life that can be represented as alternative ways of experiencing the world. The atmosphere of these alternatives is determined by very deep commitments, passions, or enthusiasms. And, Kierkegaard says, one does not flippantly move from style to style. The process of transformation is usually painful, akin to birth—a terrifying leap, where security cannot be guaranteed.

Kierkegaard, however, tends also to view life-styles as stages—closely related to each other within a process of maturation. More mature stages do not abolish the less mature, but are subsumed and given a new spirit by the higher commitments. For example, Kierkegaard (a fairly orthodox Protestant) sees man's highest development to be in the Christian experience, but this experience does not destroy the "aesthetic" or the "ethical" stages through which the pilgrim may have passed. These are still present, yet experienced in a new, re-energized fashion.

In the formative process of middle-class social character, there is a kind of logic that leads from what we will call savage styles, through conscientious styles, to the expansive life pattern. Savage styles simply cannot provide a stable frame of reference within the American suburb, so savage styles usually coexist with the conscientious. The union constitutes what most of us identify as the stereotyped behavior of the average suburbanite: patriotic, sometimes reactionary, concerned about ideals and about living the consistently virtuous life, hardworking, and fearful of moral and social decay. The conscientious man occasionally acts in a savage manner, and vice versa.

Likewise, the expansive radical does not absolutely repudiate or destroy the savage and conscientious patterns. He experiments with them. Savage arts, acts, and beliefs are acknowledged and enjoyed for what they are; conscientious belief systems are given their place. But the expansive man is in control. He is the free man, who can dabble with styles that his neighbors take absolutely seriously.

Savage Styles

Savage styles in the suburb are related to what Ernst Cassirer calls the mythical mentality. This mentality, as Cassirer says, "sprouts forth from deep human emotions," [20] particularly from "the deep desire of the individual to be freed from the fetters of its individuality, to immerse itself in the stream of universal life, to lose its identity, to be absorbed into the whole of nature. . . ." [21] The savage style grows out of loneliness—the experience of persons who feel their weakness and isolation in the face of threatening events and mysterious forces. It is far from being a style that is prehuman, an orgy of frightened emotions akin to the wail of the sloth as it falls into the tar pits. Instead, the mythical mentality is highly sophisticated in its own way, being a satisfying means of operating in situations where more rational means seem to be absent.

The mythical mentality, then, should not be understood as a style that is useful in any and all circumstances. Even in primitive societies, where it tended to govern much of man's social experience, it did not consistently operate at the same level of intensity. The anthropologist Bronislaw Malinowski, for example, observed that in the Trobriand Islands, magic and myth were employed only when persons had to deal with situations that were either so complex or so overwhelming as to exclude commonsensical strategies. The mythical mentality was strictly circumscribed, and most of the time primitive man cast his fate with his own ingenuity in using technical means to solve problems. To illustrate, Malinowski describes the Trobriand native's activity in producing an implement: "He is strictly empirical, that is, scientific, in the choice of his material, in the manner in which he strikes, cuts, and polishes the blade. He relies completely on his skill, on his reason and his endurance. There is no exaggeration in saying that in all matters where knowledge is sufficient the native relies on it exclusively." [22]

Malinowski's observations apply equally well to the American suburb. Most of the time and in most activities, suburbanites operate in a fairly pragmatic, practical manner, utilizing chemicals to make their lawns green, vitamins to make their children healthy, and mathematics to make their space probes function. Savage styles emerge in the face of bafflement, hurt feelings, civil disorder, threats to collective security, and the whims of fate or nature. On these occasions, any casual observer could notice the mythical mentality in full swing—the endeavor to meet threats through the assertion that one's defenses include the strength of the whole mysteriously united tribe, and sometimes the strength of strange and magical rites.

I, the Tribe

In May, 1969, for example, Negro City Councilman Thomas Bradley was defeated in his race for the position of mayor of Los Angeles in spite of the fact that all polls showed him to be far in the lead. Post-election analysts were generally in agreement that it was a fear of militancy and a frightened response to civil violence that finally cemented a white bloc, even though Bradley had consistently disaffiliated himself from extremist factions. Los Angeles' suburban behavior here followed the classic savage pattern. The tribe, as if receiving the signal from on high, knew that it was One, a mystical unity, with a cause to defend and an outsider to be opposed. The white tribe voted white (just as the black tribe, defensively, voted black).

The problem with savage styles in suburban conflict is, of course, that they constitute holy wars. What might be the normal irritations of suburban interaction take on a cosmic, religious significance and resist being handled casually. The mission of the youth culture, for example, is not simply to negotiate with recalcitrant parents who may or may not operate with different sets of values. Quickly, the matter shifts ground and becomes a sort of apocalyptic duel, with the youth tribe fighting for the godly values of freedom against collective representations of the Establishment, and the Establishment tribe speaking for the deities on behalf of decency, experience, and law and order. In sharpest contrast to the playful individualism of expansive man, the savage responds to external threat by losing himself in a cause, finding his strength in the awareness that he is acting on behalf of a larger whole.

Savage struggles in the suburbs resist low-key compromises. These struggles masquerade as conflict over issues that have possible solutions; but when solutions are proposed and implemented, new divisive issues inevitably arise. The reason is that the issues really are secondary to the cosmic clash between tribes, and tribes cannot afford to let divisive issues disappear. Their very survival depends on the frustrating circumstances out of which tribal unities are formed.

Because social mobility is a prime value, the expansive style thrives on peace—the circumstance that enables the suburban radical to experiment with life possibilities in a relaxed manner. Expansive man cannot operate freely when his eclecticism comes in contact with issues that have assumed savage significance. He may enjoy the experience of holy wars, the exhilaration that accompanies the struggle, but his eclecticism makes him a likely dropout from tribal causes and puts him into ultimate opposition to the taut savage stance. In the matter of peace, the savage and expansive styles do not enjoy a harmony of interest.

In the tribal wars of suburbia, the collective desires of the tribe can become personified in the shape of a hero, a leader, or a splinter political party. Then the furies of fear and mythical wish become embodied and the tribe finds in its leadership a way of picturing its own corporate personality. So, for example, the boxing career of Jerry Quarry very quickly assumes savage importance. He is a white heavyweight in a predominantly black trade, and his matches have the air of barbaric battles—race against race. As one avid Quarry watcher comments, "Two black fighters facing each other don't create the crowd excitement of a white versus a black, which, of course, is nothing new." [23] Quarry agrees. "If you have a white heavyweight who can punch, you'll always have someone to fight." [24]

In the process of granting tribal charisma to a hero or

leader, traditional bonds, which in a democratic society supposedly hold persons together (the Constitution, the law, the concern for mutual well-being), diminish in their usefulness. What grows is the magic of the hero, whose will serves as a source of tribal unity. Thus, savage styles explain the surprising process in which suburbanites become furious about how the leaders of other tribes ignore legal processes and traditional authority, while applauding similar practices among their own heroes. John Wayne, the perennially youthful movie hero, for example, builds box-office appeal by playing characters who are loose with the law in the name of a higher righteousness. A governor speaks about the value of local control of the public schools, while curtailing state aid to punish a particular urban school district for its injudicious use of public funds. A youth tribe bewails the brutal behavior of a mayor in suppressing protest, while its own leaders catcall in order to make it impossible for a commencement speaker to address his audience. The popular singer becomes something of a folk hero in spite of, or because of, the fact that he is associated with images of gangsterism. In tribalism, leadership is by definition above the law, because the savage heritage grants it the function of supplying a new form of social cohesion—of being itself the source and arbiter of law.

Ironically, expansive man enjoys the savage heroes also. He will buy their records, see their movies, go to their fights, and vote their tickets, simply because the savage heroes are such fascinating individuals—interesting "crooks." They have color and verve. They are atrocious, more like cartoons than serious possibilities, and their presence makes the suburb a more peppery, enjoyable place. A strange coalition develops, then, to create financial and political support for the savage heroes. They are loved, but for different reasons. They are the tense embodiment of tribal fears and wishes; but outside the savage perspective, this very tension turns them into laughable objects—the source of party-time quotable quotes.

Savage Styles and Pluralism

The savage experience of tribal unity also explains, at least partially, the difficulty that the suburb has with America's experience of pluralism. The mythical understanding of the tribe makes it impossible to think of a social whole as being composed of a number of parts that conflict with one another. It precludes thinking of the American tribe, for example, as able to survive while various groups fight with one another over different visions of social justice. Such a struggle is interpreted as growing from a tribal death wish, tantamount to the destruction of collective identity.

Unfortunately, the demise of the Puritan consensus in America coincided with the height of the cold war, when a tribal mentality grew in response to the extension of Soviet influence. Just at the moment when the Supreme Court acknowledged that "separate but equal" schools produced factions with separate but unequal opportunity, when a responsible party movement was attempting to divide American parties into liberal and conservative factions, when the issue of federal aid to parochial schools seemed to rend the religious communities—the mythical mentality was demanding the mystical union required to meet the threat of international devastation. The middle class responded predictably: with a schizophrenia about pluralism. Its savages translated factionalism into terms of treason; and unconventionality virtually became synonymous with un-Americanism. Pluralism was seen as part of a plot to destroy the social union. Other suburbanites, however, saw the development of savage styles as the largest danger, seeing there analogies to the rise of Nazism and finding in them a vicious rebuttal of the liberal dream that a pluralistic society is best prepared to find truth. Even in the present period, the schizophrenia continues, contingent on the ever-strong fear of a tribal war with the Communist bloc.

The new presence, however, is the expansive style, which finds in the resistance to pluralism an ultimate threat. Savagery thrives on social agreement, but expansive man sees no virtue in consensus. He cannot believe that the pluralistic society is always on the verge of dissolution. Instead, he locates its unifying bond in diversity itself—in the agreement to let styles compete within a system that respects the rules of the game. For expansive man, the most sharply defined pluralism is the most healthy. It is the social analogue to his own personality.

Savage Sensuality

The mythical mentality assigns great importance to the sensuous sacred ritual, and claims all the faculties of the individual. If, from the perspective of persons outside the tribal framework, the savage style appears superficial and less intellectually demanding, that is only because it is so multidimensional. Savagery demands doctrinal loyalties. But it also has its love beads, the woolly clothes, the holiday pageants, the careful observance of verbal amenities, the posters, the lodge rituals, the flag ceremonies, and the carefully calculated music. All contribute to the intense and broadly demanding world of the mythical mentality as well as to its deeply satisfying enjoyment of this world. Over and against the tribal scene, the stark lines of the classroom and the whitewashed church seem starved indeed.

But the savage world is not experienced luxuriously and freely like that enjoyed by expansive man. Instead, suburban savages operate in a controlled, nervous manner, moving through what might be enjoyed as a profusely rich round of ceremonies with an eye to the ever-present possibility of subversion. A case in point is the widely reported demeanor of a high school principal at a recent graduation ceremony. The setting: long lines of black-capped youngsters; the emotion of parents who are celebrating a major landmark in their families' lives; the green, green grass on the football field; and the pompous music. But the principal is nervous and restrained, and when the student speaker violates the ritual by making a brief statement of protest, he pulls the plug from the sound system.

From almost any perspective, the principal's behavior here is savage, and is almost the perfect dramatization of savage sensuality. Ceremonies become symbolic of the social order and are indispensable to that order; the slightest deviation must be handled with dispatch. Sacred objects, words, and rituals become so identified with the tribal spirit that they may even be experienced as part and parcel with the tribal opposition to contrasting points of view and styles of life. Patriotic ceremonies are often experienced negatively, as effective answers to social protest rather than as opportunities to bask luxuriously in the warmth of social symbols.

Savage Time

Mythical mentality has a deep need for explaining events in conspiratorial terms. For example, the more conservative savage cannot conceive of such events as the fall of China, the 1968 Democratic convention, and campus disturbances as being continuous with political, social, and economic movements—as almost inevitable at this time and place in history. There must be plans to be uncovered, coordinators to be exposed, and strategies to be thwarted. Left-of-center savages similarly look at police practices, the economic disabilities of the black community, the *in loco parentis* regulations of universities, and find there clues that point to the conspiracies of a jaded Establishment that is both racist and paternalistic in its manipulation of people.

The mythical mentality explains events by postulating a battle between the forces of good and the forces of evil (us and them), with individual decision makers playing their respective roles in the Universal Drama. Suburban savages may speak about "the laws of history," but they still need to explain *this* or *that* event. Why were *these* people involved? And why did the event take place at this particular time? To explain the particularity of history, recourse is taken to illustrations about the righteous or devious designs of decision makers—acts of will that are not capable of further interpretation.

This habit of mind is exasperating for the tribe's historically-minded neighbors. The savage seems paranoid, always looking for a Communist, an outside agitator, or an Establishment fink; always expecting that if he lets down his guard, someone will do him in. More irritating, however, is the habitual form of savage argument, which is more anecdotal than analytic, or systematically organized. Discussions about the American welfare program, for example, have a way of disintegrating into recitations about profligates who are having more and more children just to increase their welfare checks, wealthy individuals who have outsmarted welfare officials, and/or welfare workers who are cruelly dominating their clients' lives. These are the conspiracies that shape history—at least, history as it is viewed from savage perspectives.

So memories of the past become weapons in tribal wars. They are used to steel the tribal will—to keep alive the awareness of an enemy. And they become the vehicle whereby the enemy is discredited, assigned his rightful place as an instrument of the forces of social disruption. In short, the conspiratorial understanding of the past keeps suburban savages irritated. They are not encouraged to be patient with political opponents or to believe that social justice can arise out of democratic compromise. Instead, the mythical mentality explodes into demands that cannot be met in a pluralistic society, into preparations for the subversion, perhaps destruction, of enemies whose very presence constitutes a threat to tribal purity. The savage vision of history activates violent excitement likely to result in destructive social behavior.

The Political Allies of Savage Suburbanites

In the holy wars waged by suburban tribes, one can find a second group that often finds common cause with savages, but that does so out of a far different mind-set. These are persons who feel deeply about moral and religious principles and who believe that the national destiny is threatened when these are no longer cherished. They are absolutists, persons who find little need to agonize over the ambiguity of moral, or political choices, and who look upon expansive styles as flirtation with the devil. They have philosophies of life, philosophies of government, and beliefs about religion—carefully worked out and used in such a way that judgments are easily available for any and every kind of personal and social issue. The world is divided into persons who are right (i.e., those who agree) and those who are wrong. And they are often willing to destroy institutions that appear to be failing morally, politically, or religiously, in order to "save them from themselves."

This moral absolutism is usually found on the extreme right or the extreme left, but sometimes in between—wherever beliefs show themselves to be rigidly held, and wherever life-styles are unforgiving. In the early part of this century, for example, the absolutist mentality revolted against what appeared to be doctrinal and moral decay in Protestantism and walked out of the major denominations to create a multitude of splinter groups. More recently, the absolutist mentality spawned such political movements as those connected with Eugene McCarthy, Douglas MacArthur, and George Wallace. Together these constituted a highly flammable, antipragmatic brand of American politics—a brand that could not tolerate compromise and certainly could not find in compromise a positive value.

When savage tribes ally with this rigidly principled mentality, grounds are created for holocaust. The danger in the American suburb is heightened by the fact that this alliance seems to be taking on political energy. It is anachronistic to say that the suburb is cut politically into liberal and conservative factions, the issues being fought on the classic liberal-conservative lines. The real battle pits the savage-principlist coalition against a coalition of expansive men, moderate liberals, and moderate conservatives. Practically speaking, this means that the battle is between zealots and compromising pragmatists. It was not at all uncommon, for example, in 1964, to see supporters of the radical left pasting Goldwater stickers on their bumpers and, in 1968, a large number of militant blacks supporting the Wallace campaign. In the campus disorders of the late 1960's, the leftist Students for a Democratic Society could easily join forces with right-wing student groups around such issues as a volunteer army and around strategies for the disruption of gradualist college administrations.

The savage and principlist positions come to their coalition with different symbols, heroes, and ideologies, but theirs is a new kind of alliance—an alliance of similar styles rather than ideologies. They share the absolutist reaction against gradualist political behavior and they can express their frustration with the politics of compromise. Together, this assortment of rightist and leftist groups constitutes the most viable politically revolutionary potential in the suburb. They are the overreactors, and thereby they are the basis for a fundamentalist, disruptive political movement.

Measured against the playful politics of expansive man —a politics that has more to do with responding piecemeal to events, with projecting images, and with pragmatism than with traditional political philosophy—a new stylistic definition of conservatism appears to be in the making. The "new conservative" is the ideologue in politics, and the new reactionary front (the extremist group) is made up of persons who feel so strongly about the so-called American principles, however defined, that they are willing to disrupt the political scene in order to keep it from self-destruction. Thus viewed, the New Left is the most reactionary element currently on the political horizon, fitfully emulating the behavior of frontier evangelists who called for a rebirth of principles and who hatcheted the saloons that spawned libertine moral heresies. Far from being *avant* threats to the American dream, the New Left joins hands in the stylistic revolution with the Daughters of the American Revolution, George Wallace's party, and the American Legion in defending the faith.

Chapter 5

NEIGHBORS:
THE CONSCIENTIOUS MAJORITY

OBVIOUSLY, the suburb is not now populated heavily with the brittle personalities of the new reactionary front, but the picture of principled rigidity does demonstrate the logical extreme of a mentality that probably still dominates suburbia's majority. The phrase "principled rigidity" fails satisfactorily to describe this more mellow life-style, and we have chosen rather to speak of it as the "conscientious mentality." The conscientious man usually appears to be a reasonable fellow, although sometimes, especially when threatened by overwhelming events, he lapses into savage styles. For the most part, he fits our image of the solid citizen. He tends toward the dogmatism of the new reactionary front, and can feel himself slipping either toward the right or the left. But his common sense generally keeps him at a moderate-to-liberal position. He is more in danger of being cheerfully drab than of jolting his neighbors by unpredictable moves.

The Self as Hierarchy

The conscientious man, unlike the expansive man, still thinks of himself according to the hierarchical image, which he inherited from the ancient world. At the very top—the highest in man—are the spiritual and mental capabilities. Indeed, man is set apart from the beasts and the vegetables by virtue of the fact that he can think, inquire after truth, and enjoy moments of spiritual illumination. According to the conscientious mentality, that man can worship may well be his crowning dignity. But this same dignity is affirmed in the scientific quest for understanding, in the mathematician's ability to quantify relations in his universe, and in man's desire to discover the nature of the moral law. It is more humanly fulfilling to be a lawyer than to be a bricklayer, to be a professor than to be a weightlifter.

The scale ranges downward, assigning a reduced dignity to those capabilities and activities which are "mixed" with the physical. Thus, although the conscientious suburbanite may thoroughly enjoy professional football and baseball, he still feels that the extraordinarily high salaries there are a bit immoral. He is absolutely convinced that expansive man's body-awareness experiences and nude swimming are ways of getting cheap sexual thrills ("better to limit that sort of thing to the privacy of your own home"). His wife feels dissatisfied with the housework and wants to get a job so she can use her mind. If she never completed college, she feels inadequate beside her well-educated husband. Both conscientious man and his wife will do almost anything to ensure that their offspring get the best education possible; and in the face of student unrest, they are certain that they know what that best possible education is.

The hierarchical understanding of selfhood leads to a vastly different relation to the physical than that experienced by the expansive mentality. Expansive man is increasingly able to appreciate physically oriented happenings, and he does not try to find morals, symbolic meanings, truths, or lessons in the world of the senses. He does not utilize the physical for purposes outside the physical—as, for example, enjoying nature in order to glorify God, or taking children outside to look at the stars in order to get an idea of the eternal order. Difficult as it is to express, the expansive mentality believes that a certain violation occurs when the "logic" of the physical is translated into other forms—sentences, mathematical formulas.

But the same is not the case with the conscientious mentality, although conscientious suburbanites have developed a variety of ways for handling the physical. One group, for example, tirelessly investigates the meaning of the physical. When telling his adolescent children about the birds and the bees, a member of this conscientious group will speak about how the sex act is symbolic of love and duty. At the art gallery, he will look for the point of abstract art. He will want to know what a symphony is trying to say. And he will even ask his wife (in rare poetic moments) about the meaning of love. In other words, the physical universe is practically experienced as a vast collection of objects, the fun of which is in letting them point beyond themselves to another universe of meanings. Experiencing the physical world is like going to a drama, where every motion is likely to provide fruitful ground for symbolic interpretation.

Another conscientious group will look upon nature as a mystery to be understood, a chaos to be conquered, a vast resource to be tapped for human purposes. It is restless in the face of an unexplained event or an unsolved problem. And, at an extreme, it sees little wrong with a highway through the park or oil wells along the coastline. It finds the main value of space probes in the opportunity afforded for the development of technological skills. And when conscientious individuals travel, they are interested in the economic potential of various areas.

A third group is conscientious about nature itself—a mentality that provides a healthy basis for conservation crusades, Sierra Clubs, and the tent-making industry. Nature becomes a cause: it is to be protected and enjoyed, particularly because the country's national reserves offer a simpler, rugged, unspoiled escape from the grayness of city life. The moralizing spirit is never very far beneath the surface, however, and conscientious campers have a way of looking and sounding like grown-up Boy Scouts eagerly acting out the scout oath. They have a passion for knowing the names of bushes, rocks, valleys, and geological formations, as well as for knowing the geological and social history of their recreation areas. The simplicity of camping life is experienced as a kind of moral purity, with city life playing the role of villain serpent. The enjoyment of nature is closely connected with a belief that people are better when they are closer to things that are not manufactured, and that children will grow up to be better people if they have sung songs and roasted marshmallows in front of a campfire. Knowing how to light a fire, to backpack, and to follow a compass, in spite of their almost total uselessness in the suburban environment, serve as highly charged symbols of masculine fulfillment. The natural life becomes indistinguishable from the moral life, which is really the issue in the conscientious experience of the camping movement.

Wholeness as a Moral Ideal

We have, in sum, a man who has a sense of rightness and who is aware that there is much in the world that is not right. When he looks at the life-style of expansive radicality, with its habit of tinkering with beliefs, dressing up in funny costumes, and being irreverent, the conscientious man shudders. He thinks of Pompeii and the fall of Rome. How long, O Lord, until the American suburb also falls in the wake of its moral decline?

A few years ago, one of us was teaching an introductory philosophy class to suburban youth. Inevitably, students were led down the rocky road to the insight that more than one way exists to make sense out of their world, and that different, conflicting points of view may each be relatively satisfactory. In this situation, expansive students felt liberated and were no longer ashamed of their eclecticism. But conscientious students were invariably offended. They felt that the slick young college teacher was putting something over on them, because it was only reasonable to believe that there is a single set of truths to be figured out. The teacher of philosophy is always being cast as a morally suspicious character. He tempts young students into his den and eats them up. Worse, he disillusions them.

So conscientious men are constantly trying to find what is true, and they do not like to entertain doubts that someday—perhaps in the hereafter—the truth can be known. For the present, they are content to take a few risks, making reasonable guesses about what is good and true and right. They will do the best they can. All they require is sincerity and as great a consistency as possible. In fact, that is what integrity is: being consistent.

There is the rub. What is integrity for the conscientious style is precisely that which has lost meaning for the expansive radical. The expansive style is eclectic. The conscientious man values coherence. The expansive style views the concern for consistency as an unnecessary restriction on the attempt to enjoy an enlarging set of possibilities. The conscientious man believes that the expansive individual has betrayed the fundamental discipline of the well-ordered life; that he looks sloppy and morally compromised. The expansive man usually has a good amount of the conscientious in him; yet he normally holds a number of conflicting conscientious systems together.

The concern for coherence—being a unified, whole, integrated individual—is absolutely central for the conscientious man. However he chooses to conceptualize his faith, in whatever personal, political, social, or religious terms, he will think of his life as having a vocation. And he will measure his success insofar as he is able to live up to it. Conscientious man takes very seriously Søren Kierkegaard's version of the good life, "Purity of heart is to will one thing." So conscientious man is concerned about inconsistencies and wants to get his priorities straight. The familiar image of the man who goes to church on Sunday but who forgets his religious commitments the rest of the week is offensive, because conscientious man cannot believe that it is possible to hold sincerely to more than one set of loyalties. "No man can serve two masters."

His moral ideal ultimately matches the symbol with which the conscientious man understands himself: the hierarchy, in which the spirit or the mind is in control, coordinating all dimensions of a man's life in harmony with controlling ideals. The passions, the body, sexual pleasures, although subject to occasional deprecation, are considered to have positive meaning, when they are at one with a person's overall life vocation.

The conscientious mentality expands its concern for self-fulfillment and wholeness to the social sphere, so conscientious men provide the foundation for much of the social and political activism that keeps suburbia livable. Collective alienation is the social sin that corresponds to the fragmentation of the integrated individual, the loss of personal coherence. The conscientious mentality is offended by the arbitrary exclusion of individuals or classes from what it considers to be the normal state of affairs in the body politic. And unlike his savage neighbors, conscientious man can live with a sharply pluralist society, in which conflicting factions struggle to affect national policy—as long as he can be convinced that pluralism constitutes a workable system.

Conscientiousness, steeped in the concern for social integration, breeds the liberal spirit. While making their Boy Scout treks into the wilderness, conscientious men are also providing the money and energy to crusade for the preservation of unspoiled forests and water resources. In the next decade, both savages and expansive individuals may owe their very existence to the painstaking, patient, and sacrificial efforts of such persons, who are dealing with the problems of smog, tax crises, educational reform, water pollution, and regional planning. The conscientious mentality knows that urban crises are subtle, confusing, and complex, and it is able to sustain attention long enough to deal with issues in these terms. While savages look for simple solutions (and for the conspiracies behind urban problems), and while expansive men flit in and out of causes, conscientious individuals are often looking for workable plans to provide the conditions in which persons can grow in healthy ways.

Conscientious Organizations

Conscientious man is always organizing something, from garden clubs to picket lines, fair-housing committees to planned parenthood leagues. He is on church rolls even when he does not go regularly, and often he supports organizations financially when he agrees with their purposes but cannot give his own time and effort. Without conscientious men, churches and other public service organizations would have to close up shop, because they are not likely to sustain themselves through the kind of efforts received from savages and expansive men. Even though such organizations cannot do without other mentalities, they are founded on the exhaustive efforts of a small core of conscientious personalities who are willing to identify themselves with the various enterprises or issues. Savages are very good to have on the fringes, but they are likely to split organizations in wars over picky issues such as the color of carpets, and they are likely to explode when they cannot feel sympathetic with an organization's leadership. Expansive men are too busy and refuse to be totally identified with any community, and, besides, they are easily bored with the groveling, detailed level of organizational life. So the poor, tired, conscientious population carries the load. It organizes, recruits, sweeps up, runs the mimeograph machines, teaches the classes, takes the chairmanship for an extra term because no one else will do it, and solicits for all manner of charitable fund drives. Conscientious men often get angry with their neighbors, but they plow on anyway.

Ironically, the trouble with most of conscientious man's organizations is that they are neither savage nor expansive. Communty organizers have long known that it is far easier to organize and to maintain an effort when the motive is a savage fear or hatred—far easier to organize against an enemy tribe than to organize on behalf of a positive cause. In our own suburban community, for example, neighbors had no trouble at all in mounting an effort to oppose expansion of the city's airport when outsiders (in this case, downtown businessmen) seemed to be ignoring the suburb's fear of increased noise. But in this same neighborhood, it is like pulling teeth to organize an enthusiastic P.T.A., virtually impossible to recruit a stable assemblage of church school teachers, and impossible to keep a political organization going between elections.

Expansive organizations have a way of staying strong, also, particularly when they are administered by conscientious individuals. These are organizations that often play with ritual and recognize the importance of putting money into imaginative events and atmospheres. They are customarily more recreational than political or religious, although occasionally seriously founded organizations will function in the expansive mood, especially Assistance Leagues and other fashionable charity organizations. Unfortunately, the expansive style takes money, and conscientious organizations are usually short in that department. The expansive style also takes imagination and some risk, and many conscientious organizations are short in that department, also.

The conscientious mentality, doing the jobs that a healthy society must have done, usually has a terrible time initiating and sustaining its organizations. One of us, for example, was associated during its organizational phase with an urban coalition—a community organization attempting to coalesce conscientious individuals from business, minority communities, government, education, and labor. The task assigned was typically conscientious: coordinating and initiating projects to improve the broad level of well-being in the metropolis. For over a year the board of directors and task forces struggled to define their purposes, and they were able to effect some successes. But there is still a chasm between differing concepts of the coalition, and still a feeling that if the coalition moves controversially, it will fall apart.

Conscientious personalities have a hard time agreeing on what their organizations should do—that is, when their tasks are not settled already by some large threat or by some clear self-interest (when savage styles come into play). In their organizational careers, most of them have experienced repeatedly the process of trying to work out consensuses, trying to deal with those who feel the organization is not aggressive enough or is too aggressive, and trying to keep attendance up. If the organization survives for an extended period, its stability is established not so much by the fact that agreements have been reached as by the fact that participation has either become habitual or has assumed multiple, unintended functions, such as the provision of friendships, status, business contacts, access to other positions, recreation, or opportunities to socialize the children. Conscientious leaders often bemoan this state of affairs, since to them such organizations look as though they have gone flabby. But they come to accept the fate of their lot, believing that at least they can accomplish a few of their original intentions while suffering through the folderol. Instead, they should rejoice. Their organization has been guaranteed a life-span that will not end easily. They also have at their disposal an association strong enough to encourage occasional internal reformation efforts.

But conscientious persons, more than other suburbanites, are perpetually parading their organizational failures before their own downcast eyes. Their vision, consistent with their hierarchical mentality, is of an ideal organization—controlled by ideas or commitments, around which persons are drawn together. Harvey Cox, for example, says that the Christian church, at its best, is the *laos,* the people of God, open to the changing will of God in history, unencumbered by burdensome mortgages and expensive physical facilities. The church becomes a perpetual pilgrimage to where the action is, spurred by the single commitment to be an instrument of God in effecting divine purposes.[25]

But most conscientious church folk, similar to organization men everywhere, are repeatedly disillusioned by the fact that more "physical" matters seem to dominate their collective lives. They are limited by perpetual financial inadequacies; they struggle over the color of paint in the ladies' parlor; they plan father-son banquets; they moan about the need for choir robes; and they seem more interested in bowling than in spiritual exercises. If Sunday morning worship was not a reminder of the spiritual basis for the church's presence, one would have a hard time discovering that basis from an analysis of the conversations that proceed among parishioners.

Therein lies the reason why conscientious organizers become discouraged, drop out, or gravitate to judgment movements—charismatic groups that thrive on negative judgments about the emotional poverty and absence of convictional zeal in long-established conscientious organizations. These movements come panting on to the suburban landscape, promising emotional intensity and group life dominated by inspiring ideals, and they are occasionally able to thrive—albeit briefly—to satisfy the thirst of individuals who have lost the thrill. Occasionally, also, conscientious organizations become alarmed at the vigor of judgment movements, and incorporate their contributions into their establishment styles, thus sponsoring minor reformations. Sad to say, however, judgment movements are no more exempt from the slings and arrows of conscientious fortune than those whom they judge. And within time, these settle down to the predictably "physical" habits and to the ritual of self-flagellation.

The moral of the story is that conscientious men ought to recognize that their woes are quite predictable, but that they nevertheless make their extremely valuable contributions to the humanity of American society through these claptrap, always-on-the-verge-of-collapsing organizations. Reformation movements and judgment movements are absolutely necessary to the health of conscientious organizational life, for without them it could ossify unmercifully. Yet conscientious persons ought to love their claptraps more, because there is a stability and patience there without which our society would suffer greatly.

The biggest temptation for conscientious organizations is to move in the savage direction, building enthusiasm and financial support out of irrational tribal opposition to outsiders and out of dramatizing the conspiracies that threaten social dissolution. Thriving tribes can be built out of floundering conscientious organizations, but the price is great. Savage emotions can easily be confused with sincere conscientiousness, hatred with deep belief. But finally there is nothing more destructive of the conscientious attempt to build community around rational beliefs and commitments than the holy-war atmosphere whipped up by the charismatic demagogue.

It is quite another case with the relationship of conscientious and expansive styles in the enlivenment of associations. Expansive styles are potentially destructive in their propensity to deflate convictional seriousness; they are unable to provide the stuff out of which martyrs are made. But the expansive spirit takes conscientious man seriously, appreciates his symbols, and knows about his contribution to the common good. Except for his underlying detachment, convictional humor, and lapses into eclecticism, expansive man is virtually indistinguishable from his conscientious neighbors. But the expansive style has an enormous contribution to make to those who are struggling with conscientious organizations. Expansive man can enrich, perhaps save, such organizations by reminding his fellows about the aesthetic side of group life; and he may even point the way to a new kind of revival—a revival of ethos. Things can become more interesting when expansive individuals get into offices within conscientious organizations, and the interest or excitement probably will not detract much from the organizational mission.

Put another way, expansive man can help conscientious man to get rid of his hierarchical ideal and to see that his values really are not in tension with the "physical" elements that have been cast into the demon role. Expansive styles can show that conscientiousness has not erred in falling into "physical" activities. Conscientious men simply have not known how to pull off a decent organizational party, or how to bask in an environment that appeals to all the faculties of individuals. Because conscientious organizations have seen the sensual and playful as their fall, they have not as yet devoted sufficient time, money, and imagination to the bodies (including the heads) of their members. Expansive members might well be encouraged to come from the back rows to the circle where the decision makers sit, because, happily, there is a coincidence of interest between expansive and conscientious neighbors.

Conscientious Time

Conscientious men often appear to start every day as if it were the first day of history, or at least the day immediately following the sad fall of Adam and Eve in the Garden of Eden. They gather around tables to deal with the woes of injustice, assuming that these have only recently been discovered and that no intelligent effort has as yet been expended to find solutions. Or they try to figure out how to deal with the problems of violence in their cities or of the morality of warfare, not even feeling guilty about their vast ignorance of how a succession of perceptive minds has considered similar issues in the past. In part, the reason for this astonishing ahistorical behavior is that conscientious men are utterly convinced that contemporary social, economic, and political issues are so unique that little can be derived from past example. But, more important, the conscientious mentality tends to work in a historical vacuum because it is problem-oriented rather than extended toward either the past or the future. This mentality, at first blush, seems more oriented toward the future than the past, but first impressions here are deceptive. Conscientious men usually look on their vocations, individual and collective, as a set of situations in which commitments and purposes ought consistently to be implemented. The spirit is one of becoming, yet the becoming is in a perpetual now.

Several years ago, for example, one of us was invited to join a group of conscientious individuals, under the auspices of a national organization, to consider problems of economic justice, work, and leisure in the technological society. The most impressive thing about the group was who had been invited: representatives from various sectors of the economy, representatives from the sponsoring organization, and two professional social moralists. There were no historians, presumably because no one thought about inviting one. And partially as a result, the subsequent two years of discussion suffered irreparably, devoid of perspective, deprived of the wisdom of even the past fifty years. The study group developed a surprisingly effective report considering the circumstances, but as far as we know, an equally ahistorical public no longer knows of the document's existence. Surely we were not called together for the purpose of entertaining ourselves, but that is the impression the experience left. We started on the brink of history, and now other committees meet in the same rooms without knowing about the lofty thoughts we generated there. They too belong to the first generation.

The situation is tragic, because if conscientious man does not maintain a serious sense of participation in the process of history, no one else in suburbia will. Expansive man makes his contribution through his nostalgic style; he enjoys history in the form of Indian yarn paintings and Martha Washington ruffles. Suburban savages use history like a club, knocking enemies over the head with ossified conspiratorial memories. It remains for the conscientious man to approach the past with curiosity, respect (yet freedom), a desire to find there a way of understanding his own identity, a feeling for the evolution of collective problems, and a sense of the context in which he will act. If it is true that the idea of history as a linear continuum, holding in tension the precedents of the past and the possibility of novelty, is a significant cultural accomplishment, the stakes are high in the conscientious habit of forgetfulness. Suburbia is in danger of losing one of the few really important ideas in the experience of the human breed, and it can lose this fragile idea without knowing what has occurred. The situation would be roughly like forgetting about the shape of the wheel, or forgetting about the possibility of fire.

The problem belongs peculiarly to the conscientious mentality, because the historical sense has been associated with the conscientious process of developing vocational communities. History belongs to communities that are evolving an identity and that bind persons together in the act of remembering their common past and projecting their common future. For example, it was not accidental that, until a few years ago, the normal pattern in the suburban junior high and senior high schools and colleges was to limit the history curriculum to courses that excluded the stories of significant social groupings. It was not until these excluded regional, national, and racial communities assumed importance for middle-class identity that their histories moved into the public domain. The history curriculum is like a middle-class social register dutifully recording which life stories are worth paying attention to—which have a right to impinge on the way we think about ourselves. The recent introduction of black and Mexican-American histories is not a rounding out of the curriculum or a response to a natural right. The courses constitute suburbia's way of announcing that, politically, the blacks and the Mexican Americans are now part of the club whose pasts have to be considered, and that they have the power of laying claim to the public schools as an instrument in forging their own self-identity.

The so-called "new history" currently being developed among innovative public educators contributes mightily to the heroic stand that suburbia must make to preserve an alive interest in the past. Historians are now saying to their students what they have said to one another for many years: that history is less a science than an art—the art of understanding the present through interpreting the past. Every age has to rewrite its history books, even if no new data has been collected, simply because historical interpretations, even the "facts" that are relevant, change as social issues are altered. The teaching of this kind of history in suburban schools is sharply different from that within which so many adults suffered. The atmosphere today is more one of self-discovery and problem-solving, and less one of rote memorization.

But the "new history" is in danger of becoming one more form of ghetto, an activity disturbingly isolated from commonplace ways of dealing with problems and of thinking about one's own identity. When students emerge from their history lessons, they are apt to move into a historical vacuum and find that the institutions where they spend their time could not care less about the past. The historical consciousness does not have a payoff. It will not help you get a job, nor will it earn you friends, nor will it make people seek your advice. It can offer a sense of being at home in the sweep of time, which is not a mean prize, but such a sense is private and not reinforced by a system of socially approved rewards.

The obligation that conscientious suburbanites carry for preserving the historical consciousness falls most heavily on middle-class politicians, educators, and churchmen. The state, the school (particularly the university), and the church are institutions where the past has left a rich deposit of symbols, practices, traditions, and rituals—for exercise; ecclesiastical ceremonies such as ordination; the ample, the highly routine procedures of the graduation expomp of judicial procedures; state funerals with riderless horses. In the light of pressures to do the jobs at hand, such practices can appear indefensible, particularly when large expenditures are concerned. But they are among the few levers available for reminding suburbanites that they stand in the succession of man and that they hold responsibility to that succession.

Part of the problem, of course, is that conscientious persons have not learned the expansive lesson that history can be luxuriously enjoyed and that this enjoyment is not antithetical to conscientious obligations. They tend to look on the ceremonies and rigid customs as irrational intrusions, stealing resources that might properly be devoted to implementing serious purposes. Actually, the symbols and the ceremonies of history are serious business, not only because they maintain a culturally important idea, but because they encourage a time-conscious mentality that grants depth and dignity to the tasks at hand. The expansive interest in building a richly decorated institutional life, as well as its playful desire to reminisce nostalgically, are instruments readily at hand in suburbia. Their appropriation ought to be a matter of primacy for conscientious persons who are looking for ways of stemming the ahistorical tides, and who are aware that the routines of middle-class institutions may well be the last really viable place for supporting the historical consciousness.

Chapter 6

PATHOLOGIES
OF THE RADICAL SUBURB

AMERICANS have always rushed into styles and move-ments with the verve of adolescence, and almost always they have suffered for it. Such is the case with the exuber-ant arrival of expansive man. He comes on the scene amid all the excitement of a culturally liberating event, full of promise and open to the future. But he also comes as the bearer of potential tragedy. As with any life process, achievements involve their own characterological patholo-gies.

We know whereof we speak. Both of us grew up and live in Greater Los Angeles, where—as Pauline Kael ob-serves from the distance of saner San Francisco—the fu-ture is embodied for all the world to see. Our great hint of things to come, which we call Los Angeles, has a script that could have been written in Erik Erikson's clinic. We invented the identity crisis here. But, be it known, we are also among the pioneers of suburban radicality. This is an exciting place to develop suburb-watching skills: first in fulfillment, first in casualties. It is here that we have be-come confirmed advocates as well as troubled doubters of the expansive ethos. Had we lived in a place where the expansive takeover is going more slowly and covertly, we might have become its buoyant champions. But in Los An-

geles we can see it in all of its sickness as well as its
promise.

The Illness of Elitist Politics

Suburban radicality is a class phenomenon. It is a style
that grows in elitist circumstances, simply because only an
economic elite can afford the events and objects that constitute the necessary expansive environment. And only an
elite can have the leisure and the social mobility to allow
for that time-consuming, territory-hopping round of expansive activities. Money is the key.

The elitist assumptions of cultural radicality become obvious in any survey of the suburban shops that cater to expansive tastes. On the western edge of Los Angeles, for
example, there is a group of clothing stores that serve
radicals from Beverly Hills, Bel Aire, and Hollywood. If a
radical wants to find here the garb of a social dropout, he
cannot do so for less than one hundred dollars. Some of
the shops carry an abundant supply of antique shoes (apparently shipped in from Salvation Army warehouses)
and even racks of scraped and torn leather jackets.
But the prices are not those of the thrift shop variety. It takes money to drop out. Likewise, radical garb
of the playful, nostalgic, sensual type is frightening in its
cost.

But one does not have to go indoors to discover the
elitist assumptions of expansiveness. In Los Angeles, a
person has only to saddle up his automobile and drive
across the metropolis on any major artery. To no one's
astonishment, he will find that a very large percentage of
the city is decaying; that the schools are in need of paint;
that, except for isolated pockets of affluence, the middle
class has deserted the city. When he drives through areas
surrounding downtown, he will make certain that his auto-

mobile doors are locked, because he knows full well that the areas are suffering from high crime rates. In short, a trip across the city makes one glad to return to the suburb. But the suburb takes on an isolated feeling—out of touch with the larger failures of our society.

Expansive society is exploitative. Marxist myths, when applied to the middle-class radical, are accurate in pointing out how his fun is secured at the expense of underprivileged populations. Expansiveness comes at a high cost: undersupported city services, illiberal tax schedules, starved public resources, and irrational approaches to problems of urban education, air pollution, mass transportation, and public housing. More threatening, this exploitative relation to metropolitan society is a pale reflection of the larger international situation, where dabbling, expansive styles exist within a very, very small affluent island—isolated ideologically and emotionally from the devastating economic deprivation of whole areas of the world. The excitement of expansiveness seems grotesque when viewed against the background of international hunger.

Consequently, we must speak out of both sides of our mouth. Our liberal angers ought not to blind us to the fact that suburbia is doing a culturally significant task—that middle-class America can rightly boast about its experimentalism with life-styles. Middle-class white is beautiful. Yet, this experimentalism rests on an insensitivity to the conditions of its metropolitan, national, and international context. Expansiveness is both suburbia's greatest glory and its most subtle form of social sinfulness.

To be sure, expansive politics should not be confused with the defensive white nationalism of prominent reactionary associations. These tend to look at urban needs as the fruit of conspiracy, laziness, or lack of public pride. They are chauvinistic organizations whose pride in middle-class achievement can easily become a sick form of class indulgence. They provide an ugly cartoon of community self-congratulation, and end in a rigid opposition to most kinds of reform.

But the radical suburb cannot avoid being mistaken for white chauvinism. The radical style, with notable exceptions (which we will speak about later), persistently presents the face of indifference, especially with regard to domestic politics. Expansive men often overwhelm urban activists with their silence and frustrate politicians with their refusal to undergo the discipline of understanding social ills. Thus, in the 1960's, the suburb assumed an image of collective guilt: racist, resistant to change, self-protective.

The reason expansive man appears indiscriminately conservative, though, is not that he is guilty of all these heinous crimes. The problem is that the style belongs ideally to periods and places that are relatively peaceful and that do not divide persons along emotionally charged economic lines. The expansive agenda is not suited to an atmosphere of social reform because the response of the radical to political tension is almost inevitably irritation. His irritation is like that of the university student who must interrupt his campus frolics to go into the Army. His anger is not ideologically based, but arises out of being interrupted in the midst of an extremely satisfying round of activities. More than anything, most radicals would like to pretend that urban crisis is not real.

For savages (of the political left), expansive man's suburban whirl can be interpreted as a conspiracy. Strange, they claim, that the radical suburb should appear just at a time when American metropolitan problems have assumed such foreboding shapes. Could expansiveness merely be the slippery way in which the middle class avoids facing its civil guilt and its obligation? Could suburban society be deceiving itself—thinking of itself as awfully modern while actually playing the oldest reactionary game in the book?

Occasionally, however, the expansive style finds room for revolution. The children of expansive men are especially prone to revolution, because they sicken of their family's amorphous style and start the search for something more substantial, something that seems more moral. Thus, for example, some suburban students take on the dress and linguistic habits of black and Chicano revolutionaries; they symbolically join a tribe where personal fallibility and mortality are subsumed under a strong and lasting reality. Suburbanites seldom get a taste of permanence, but not having lost the appetite, they latch on to a seemingly lasting cause. And they can become the most ferocious revolutionaries of all.

We are not suggesting that revolutionism is in itself a pathological state of mind. Rather, we believe that expansive man can make revolutionary movements sick when he invades their precincts with his unsteady character, looking for tribal stability rather than programmatic social change. That is, we are suggesting that expansive man, who tires of his unique radical style, does not (usually) completely leave his expansiveness behind him. He is still playing around, and he ends up making revolution into another poolside game.

Expansive man therefore comes off looking exceedingly fickle and irresolute in the eyes of exploited peoples. He will not stand by to finish the revolutionary projects that mystify him. *They* want bread and butter as well as moral programs; *he* wants paradise. His participation in revolutionary groups becomes a destructive presence; he is high on rhetoric but tends to employ a suburban-parish beanbake attitude toward strategies. And so, we believe, expansive man's chronic playfulness raises the rage level in our body politic, and takes on pathological proportions.

Moreover, expansive man's falls are not necessarily leftward. To work out his hankering for a clear-cut self-image, what better direction to go than to the Right? The usual liberal wisdom would have it that movements of reaction are entirely populated by fundamentalist types—savages or grim-faced conscientious men. From our perspective, though, the suburban radical with his penchant for nostalgic play, romantic poetry, and camp art can, under stress, easily flip to right-wing causes that imaginatively connect him to "the days when"—to the days when man was in a state of unity with neighbors and earth. Living in the suburbs, the radical is routinely subjected to many of his neighbors' rightist attitudes. His normal life-style is individual and lonely, and when the need for security pushes in on him, he readily moves toward the nearest conscientious society or savage tribe. And as the hard and committed revolutionaries of the Left send rhetorical signals from downtown, indicating that they are planning an assault on his privileged territory, there is all the more reason for expansive man to move right. Verbal attacks on his property rights, his daughter, his sailboat, and his cocker spaniel can be just too much for expansive man.

Operating on a hyperrationalist world view, liberal commentators are at a loss these days to describe how college-educated people can convert to reaction, almost as if law-and-order rites were viable only for those of low I.Q. Such views are drastically shortsighted, and they altogether overestimate the ability of reason to deal with the insecurities created by the emergent expansive style. In critical situations, liberal reasonableness hardly holds a candle to the power generated by rightist visions of organic union among men of the tribe, with nature, and even with the will of the gods. Thus, in times of civil and national stress, when normal pressures are compounded unmercifully, rightist causes grow, and they are inevitably peopled by suburban radicals who simply cannot maintain their eclectic game in the face of broadly extended cultural instability.

The Expansive Quest for Immortality

In a remarkable study of the Chinese cultural revolution of the 1960's, Robert Jay Lifton finds that Mao Tsetung's pathetic need for a sense of immortality was one of the primary factors in fanning the tribal violence of the Red Guard. As an old man facing death, but robbed of a metaphysical faith that would enable aspirations to life eternal, Mao needed the comfort of identification with a deathless cause. There, in the Communist Revolution, was his hope; and when the revolution revealed signs of going flabby, it had to be hardened. It could not be allowed to die.[26]

If Mao's performance can be accepted in any way as archetypal, the age of expansiveness might well become the age of perpetual political revolution in America. Although it appears absurdly overdrawn, at first glance, to project a primary causal relation, the need for a sense of cosmic continuity does seem to bear explosive political possibilities. All of us are aware that organizations serve multiple functions, and that among these functions is that of providing symbols of identity for participants. Anyone who has been involved more than superficially in the activity of an organization knows that certain persons come to need the institution too much. They see themselves as embodiments of the cause; and the fate of the cause becomes their own life story. When individuals turn to causes to find substitutes for immortality, the stakes are raised considerably. As in Mao's case, it may appear that even a ruthless violence is worth the price, if identity-giving and life-giving missions can thereby remain energized.

Lifton's point provides the occasion for exploring expansive man's quest for immortality—a quest that is founded on a serious problem, and one that ultimately can lead in surprising directions. Expansive man knows that as surely as he celebrates the perennial youth of his style, he must die. This unhappy knowledge is not a systematic concept for him, nor is it the philosophical resignation that hog-killing farmers might have. Expansive man's awareness of mortality is hazily intuitive, and somehow it cannot be clarified within his playful style. While building his environment out of the changing possibilities of suburban experience, he suffers a collapse of imagination when it comes to picturing the end of the game. He lacks the equipment to substitute for his loss of imagination. And there are serious consequences. Things happen to him, because, after all, he does know he must die.

"Death . . . comes but once for every man," says the hero of Robert Bolt's *A Man for All Seasons,* whose stubborn stance in the face of mortal threats represents the antithesis of expansive behavior. Sir Thomas More knows who he is, where he begins and ends; and he feels that this knowledge will not change with the coming of new social arrangements. He is a conscientious man who has succeeded. His cultural universe lets him view the world as a cohesive system made concrete in Christ, church, and pope —a view that gives him a personal location, an intuition of connectedness with forces greater than himself, and a certain feeling of immortality.

What cultural world does expansive man possess to view and to find himself in? He has a *new* world, a pluralistic world, a world of his own construction. And opting to live with this fragmented world, his character takes on the quality of running water. He forsakes the commitment to permanence—an act that aggravates for expansive man the existential problem of death. Unlike his savage and conscientious neighbors, he has chosen not to depend on the conventional bearers of immortality. Myth, tribe, national perdurance, religion, moral athleticism, and reason have all at different times provided men with some degree of confidence in the extended future. But the radical cannot permanently and consistently depend on any of these.

The mythical and religious mentalities have historically been the most effective in maintaining confidence in immortality. In his book *The Philosophy of Symbolic Forms,* Ernst Cassirer indicates that for mythically-minded men, the presence of tribesmen who have passed on is so strongly sensed that the fact of death is almost denied.[27] For religious man, the sense of immortality grows out of confidence in divine sovereignty, and he extends himself in time through identification with a continuing community of faith and with the deity.[28] If the vitality of mythical and religious symbolism dims, proofs of immortality are required and elaborate arguments are developed. But, although having value for persons who are already within the community of faith, the proofs fail to be convincing. They take on the character of logical exercises; and clear-minded critics have had little difficulty in demonstrating how the conclusions about immortality do not necessarily follow from the posited premises.

Expansive man would have to alter his style drastically in order to commit himself permanently to any of these traditional means of dealing with mortal inadequacy. To really ride with his experience, he cannot go narrow. Like the exuberant Sophists of antiquity, expansive man wants to juggle the entire booming world of diverse phenomena, thereby evolving a mentality that is responsive to the facts of our era, where man no longer knows, quite literally, whether or not he has a future. It is a mentality that is also consistent with suburbia's economy, which continues to prescribe a changing world built on the axiomatic obsolescence of every human product.

By our lights, the expansive tendency to avoid a direct consideration of the problem of immortality constitutes a health-sustaining mechanism. But it is a strenuous game the radical plays, this juggling act. Never quite making a heroic stand against death, he ends in fighting bush wars

against death in every moment. One result of the refusal to
identify with conventional paths to immortality is the propensity to look for quick sips of the eternal: an evening of
sensitivity, with its insight into the ultimacy of human relationships; an inspiring religious book (preferably Eastern, written by a Westerner); a weekend trip to the Grand
Canyon to behold the permanence of nature, or short of
that, a stroll in Griffith Park; dabbling with tarot; trying an
older church; meditation. Expansive man is working out
his thirst for immortality through these innocent games.

Property, also, can be a source of immortality for one
who is battered by the demands of his style. He can settle
down and make a fetish of his book collection, his house,
his lot on the banks of the Colorado River, his stereo.
What was previously for him another diversion, and what
for less radical persons might merely be a component
within an integrated life is now made central and grim, as
if it were a matter of life and death. Little wonder that
there is hardly an issue in suburbia more calculated to produce emotional lightning than the property tax!

If the first victim of this exhausting search for immortality surrogates is expansive man himself, other persons are
inevitably involved—particularly those whose own sense of
immortality is threatened by the presence of the playful
radical. Consider, for example, the effect of his presence
within suburban Roman Catholic parishes. Here, in these
islands of immortality, playfulness can easily be interpreted as a wild form of nihilism. It looks heretical and
wayward to traditionalists, and not serious to progressives. Most of these Catholics have grown up expecting
eternal life from their church, and expansive man threatens
their expectations. He has a casualness about the symbols
of connectedness. He does not seem capable of fighting the
conventional right-left battles, largely because he quickly
becomes bored with what he regards as morbid commitments either to the nineteenth century (old immortality) or

to the coming Kingdom (new immortality). He is not easily marshaled into any cause; and he is usually unwilling to fight either for the reformation of, or for the venerable *status quo* of, parochial schools. It is a moot question whether he infuriates his Knights of Columbus friends or his liberal *Commonweal* friends more. When times get rough, both wish he would go away somewhere, and they both are capable of vicious attacks on his "spineless" ways that subvert the serious symbols of permanence. In other words, if he plays his mentality out in an uncritical manner, he can bring down fury on his head, sick fury. The situation is tragic for American Catholicism, because it is expansive man who may be able to bring the church intact into the post-modern world of guiltless pluralism. He has a talent for evoking Catholicism's impressive expansive potentialities, and he is best not chased away too soon.

There is an almost inviolate law that human institutions and organizations have as their first function self-preservation. So expansive man's counter-immortality behavior becomes extremely threatening to those who locate their own immortality in institutions that are intended to last forever. For example, the suburban radical who keeps life interesting by changing job commitments as often as possible can be regarded as subversive by empire builders. And the Lakewood couple that dramatically switches its child-raising philosophy can be an especially painful presence to other couples who are building their families on models of stability. The post office and the fire and police departments offer more examples. The growing presence of expansive employees ("just on the payroll") who are not fervent about the preservative symbols, who in varying degrees fall out of uniform, and who do not operate out of a navel-level, swamping attachment to the department and therefore do not seem so ruthlessly loyal to the department name: these individuals may do as much to unleash the forces of reaction and repression in their colleagues as do the more overt, hard revolutionaries. And they will be the first to suffer because of their "disloyalty."

Expansive Identity Crises

In the second half of the 1960's, "identity" became a word charged with revolutionary political import. Now identity refers not only to personal, existential struggles for self-measurement; it also is used in speaking about the goals and anguish of great, mass bodies. And in both the personal and collective senses, the assumption is usually made that people *ought* to have identity—some form of stable self-perception that will reliably serve persons or groups in tomorrow's struggles. This-same-me, if I have a good identity, can be counted upon. Or, if I give the impression of having a bad identity, the thing to do is to discover my true, good identity, and hold on to it.

In the standard understanding of the term, identity rests upon a static view of individual and collective personality. The process understanding that is so fundamental to Erik Erikson's view, and to the expansive style, does not seem to have been accepted by large numbers of people. And even expansive man often finds himself with serious feelings of guilt, because he lives a life of sin against the old ideal of integrity—that is, the ideal of stable, coherent life systems. The unique burden of his style is that he is tempted to return to what he thinks his ancestors had in the city: integrity, commitment, identity. In the suburb he is no longer an Irishman or an Italian, a Yankee or a Southerner, Jew or Lutheran, conservative or liberal. He is every style, in succession and all at once. In brief, the radical suburb has not yet evolved the symbols and emotions to legitimate its own mentality. The ethos of experience, which includes changing environments and changing identities, produces guilt. The enjoyment of change is tempered by fear—a fear of flying apart.

Our radical attempts to allay this fear in many ways. One is the search for leaders who seem to embody integrity. The suburban popularity of Eugene McCarthy in 1968 is an example, as is the enormous popularity of Ronald Reagan. While their political philosophies represent the established conservative-liberal poles, their emotional appeal to nostalgic memories of the days when democracy was pure are remarkably similar. Their followers gain vicarious integrity through these men who, in the public mind, seldom if ever compromise.

Another common route is a sort of overwhelming domesticity. When radicals feel guilty about their desire to change jobs, homes, sports, and churches along with their self-definitions, they often use family as the locus for their one, integral act of will. Then family outings, children's activities, station-wagon involvements, uniform clothes, wrestling, homework together—all are enjoyed with a vengeance. Sometimes this enjoyment leads to dropping out of any but employment contacts with "the world." In taking these practically monastic vows to his family, an expansive man can feel committed. Of course, his integrity can be his children's or his wife's slavery. For example, if he flings himself into domesticity concurrent with his children's teen-age motions into expansiveness (largely following the paths he has exemplified and opened for them), his search for integrity can lead to family holocaust.

Or in the search for his identity, the suburban radical can turn voluntary associations into savage tribes, where the spirit of cooperation is mutated (temporarily) into noncritical involvement. And the odd thing we find in this tribalism is that it is periodic; it does not entirely enclose expansive man's life, and therefore is all the more pernicious because he does not tire of it. It does not bore him, because he maintains other diversions.

NASA, for example, has mythical qualities for some ex-

pansive men who are hungry for integrity. Normally playful individuals can become hysterical when suggestions are
made that their team, NASA, is too costly, too luxurious
in the light of starving populations and terrific earthly traf-
fic problems. And this hysteria transcends understandable
pocketbook protectiveness. Simply the vicarious integrity
of supporting that fantastic team can be enough to turn
men savage in its behest. Yet NASA-phils, like most post-
modern savages, are not really mythically-minded; they do
not find cosmic integrity in their love; they have other interests. The cohesion of the NASA team does offer a powerful model of integrity, but except for the automatons
who give their full time to the team, it remains largely an
entertainment for most—savage entertainment, but without the beauty and comfort of true myth. There is a special
sickness, we think, in expansive individuals who, to gain
integrity, will fight wildly to defend not the gods, but what
they themselves know is more on the Disneyland level.

Another example might be the recent appearance of associations committed to deadly diversions. Expansive man,
lacking a reliable means of legitimating his own noncom-
mittal life, can, in critical moments, find integrity via participation in hastily formed groups which are intent upon
slitting throats to avenge evil in God's name. It was easy
for expansive men in 1964 to scoff at the inquisitorial Joe
McCarthy era. But now the eagles are flying back in. The
House and the Senate, the Subversive Activities Control
Board, and countless other groups around the country are
all intent on discovering "enemies." Expansive man likes
to participate in grand entertainment that offers no long-
term risks to himself, and he is especially susceptible to
integrity-giving entertainment. Thus, we worry about his
choices in these next few years. Over against the devil, expansive man can feel virtuous for the first time. And until
he has a rationale—an acceptable theory for affirming his
process understanding of the self—he will be prime bait

for the hateful tribalism present among us. Whether of the Right or the Left, he will be open to supreme reaction, which means that he will be reacting out of self-hatred and guilt.

Even if the radical does not move to savage extremes, his search for integrity may lead to other forms of behavior that can create no end of trouble for suburban institutions. Persons who are uneasy about their identity and who cannot legitimate the fluid character processes that belong to their style are uncomfortable in the institutions that have traditionally been identity-establishing: family, civil community, church, and school. They experience a vague sense that things are not right (that is, things are too rigid and paternalistic); and they keep these institutions in a perpetual state of unrest through their interminable criticism and their demands for privilege. Parents of adolescent youth have long been familiar with this behavior pattern, and they have known that their gangling children will sooner or later become a source of pain. The pattern is both inevitable and healthy, because the adolescent is thereby able to assert his independence. But can institutions stand the strain when affluence makes adolescents of large portions of the public, youth and adult alike? Can institutions survive in a period when their everyday activity comes under adolescent scrutiny, and when their every move is measured for signs of intolerable rigidity?

The paradox of the situation is that expansive man's dependence on identity-granting institutions grows as he resists their authority. Mature parents of adolescent youth know that they must be flexible and willing to reform authority relationships. Yet they also know that rebels grow best within parameters. The expansive style likewise cannot flourish in an environment where institutions are collapsing and where authorities grant every rhetorically expressed whim. The style requires institutions that (healthily) are able to engender competing life possibilities and to embody these in substantial ways within the behavior of various social groupings. Otherwise, expansiveness becomes destructive of the very possibilities that it enjoys.

The frightening prospect is that Americans will misunderstand what is happening to their institutions as expansiveness arrives on the scene, and will react in extreme and insensitive ways. On the one hand, the whole process can easily be transformed into a huge conscientious occasion, where the rights, privileges, and freedom of individuals are viewed in all their metaphysical grandeur. Meeting the demands and criticisms of uneasy suburban radicals can become a symbolic act in itself, an act whereby one demonstrates either his modernity or his passion for justice. But the response does not succeed, because expansive man is more interested in testing his identity-giving institutions than he is in specific reforms. The champion of expansive rights is a prime candidate for disillusionment, because there is nothing he can give away that will satisfy radical desires. Perhaps he should refrain from equating virtue with expansive demands and assume the role of one who sees value in perennially negotiating the shape of permissions and parameters.

On the other hand, when expansive persons rebel against their institutions, others are prone to draw battle lines, and grounds are prepared for a holy war. Perhaps the greatest danger to American society in the coming of expansive man is this possibility: that he will encourage a rigid, fierce polarization of the suburb, with groups uniting in a backlash to resist his disruptive behavior. The radical looks like a betrayer of the American dream, even though his style may be the optimal expression of that dream. Supposed betrayers must be eliminated, and the suburbs may well unite in socially flammable ways to rid themselves of expansive men while they are still the minority.

Our hesitations about expansive man—his politics, his poor equipment for dying, his identity crises—all are related to his ubiquity, his quality of being in more than one place at once, indeed everywhere at the same time. It is an awesome capability not customarily given to mortals who must live in history. The burden, though, for any being endowed with ubiquity is that ubiquity sometimes means that one has no home. This is what recent literature reporting God's death has told us: that the omnipresent character can end up being nowhere; he suffers from alocality. He is homeless.

Ubiquity—what a gift! Visit the giant Pickwick Bookshop in the San Fernando Valley; watch suburbanites ceaselessly swallow a waterfall of new information. Study the unprecedentedly open-ended nontradition of employment and child-raising practices among our moneyed majorities. Expansive man is acquiring a metro mind with fantastic absorptive powers not only for novel information but also for novel styles.

Too bad if he turns out to be homeless. And too bad if we all must suffer for his ubiquity.

Chapter 7

SUBURBAN SOPHISTRY:
A DEFEATED LOGIC OF PROTEST?

IN ANCIENT ATHENS, the Sophists were professional argu-ers and teachers of argument. They apparently followed the teachings of Protagoras, who suggested that "man is the measure of all things"—a bit of wisdom that has always been obscure and subject to diverse interpretations. The Sophists, however, took Protagoras to mean that political truth is relative to individual and cultural perspectives. Consequently, they gave up the attempt to find a final po-litical truth and, instead, spent their time trying arguments on for size, discovering the art of creating conviction. The commitments of sophistry were openly pragmatic, fla-grantly irrationalist, and tantalizingly experimental.

By our lights, the radical suburb, which thrives on eclec-ticism and which betrays little interest in bringing doctrinal order out of chaos, is encouraging a kind of sophist re-vival in American politics. Interestingly, both the Sophist and his suburban counterpart came to their biases by rec-ognizing the pluralism of perspectives in which persons ex-perience their political worlds. But the suburban variety is more affirmative. It does not habitually exploit clever rhe-torical devices for professional purposes; it is not identical with power politics; and it does not represent a loss of faith in the constructive possibilities of the political process. Expansive individuals, rather, are learning how to try arguments on for size, because they thoroughly enjoy discovering how things look from different perspectives. And, more important, they are beginning to sense that in the breakdown of concern for ideological consistency there are opportunities for imaginative new forms of political behavior.

Political paradox is being legitimated, and a tongue-in-cheek spirit is encouraged. With a spirit of playfulness, the radical finds himself holding together an astonishingly diverse collection of opinions, all of which he wants to defend on different occasions. "I never thought I would argue from this point of view," the middle-class sophist starts, "but here we go." And not only does he argue from the viewpoint he feels to be neglected, he argues passionately, convincingly.

A few years ago, for example, we attended a banquet at an agricultural-engineering university, where a well-known liberal had been invited to speak. The occasion was sponsored by the university's extension division, and the banquet was to be living proof that the businessmen in attendance do indeed have minds, and can even listen to a speaker whose opinions are contrary to their own. We all wondered when the explosion would come. Would the businessmen riot? Would they hiss the speaker? To everyone's amazement, though, the liberal addressed his group in the finest tradition of Calvin Coolidge. He spoke eloquently on behalf of limited government and a vital private sector, and he ended with a tribute to Adam Smith calculated to bring tears to the eyes of any red-blooded savage. Why? Later in the evening he confided that he was weary of the unskilled manner in which the conservative viewpoint is usually expressed. As an incipient pioneer of the sophist style, he had decided that—there in the ranchlands, far from his liberal colleagues—he would change his public identity, if only for an evening. He would show conservative businessmen how to argue. And, to achieve a sense of personal satisfaction, he would at last be able to show his deep sympathy for conservative beliefs, which he knew were in jangling tension with his public image.

Where does this sophistry take us? Is it healthy for a society to be so enamored with pluralism that it is in danger of losing the conviction that accompanies a narrower view? What happens to political styles in sophist territories? Who will protest when everybody can agree potentially with everything, or almost everything?

The Suburban Radical as One-Dimensional Man

At least indirectly, Herbert Marcuse's analysis of the advanced industrial society addresses itself to the cultural-political climate created by multiperspectival middle-class America. Marcuse argues that the industrial society has a way of absorbing conflicting viewpoints, legitimating them, and thereby depriving them of their critical power.[29] That is, the society can take a protesting doctrine, such as that developed by the conscientious objection movement during World War II, and can make room for it in the system (for example, it can grant military deferments). But in so doing, the society gives the protesting group a sense of self-interest in defending the *status quo,* and makes it virtually impossible to maintain the original prophetic fervor. The industrial society thus remains a pluralist society, yet the pluralism is tamed.

From Marcuse's viewpoint, then, suburban sophistry might be interpreted as what happens to people when they go "one dimensional"—when they are able to incorporate a number of political styles within their social character without allowing any one style to assume the role of prophecy. When suburbanites are able to be politically tolerant, even to think about justice in a number of ways, no one perspective may be strong enough to provide the basis for a sharp criticism of what is going on and what needs to be done. The prophetic, protesting, reforming style demands a place to stand and a way to think—a set of categories within which one habitually makes his judgments about good and evil, justice and injustice. But the suburban sophist has no place to stand. Almost by definition, he ceases to be a prophet. Like Marcuse's image of the tamely pluralistic society, the expansive personality appears to value a holding together of soft, sentimentalized perspectives, each with an interest in maintaining the collective *status quo*. Radicality appears to want the relatively harmonious coexistence of political biases, with no one bias being allowed to realize the totalitarian logic of its own development, that is, to reach the point where it demands absolute allegiance and commitment.

Protest politics have historically come from the conscientious or the savage mentality, where it is possible to find such an absolute certainty about what is good for society. Persons who see the complexity of issues and who are habitually willing to compromise do not make good crusaders. Although a stable society must have this compromising, intellectually amorphous group (otherwise it would disintegrate), it cannot look to sophists for the steam to get large-scale changes initiated. Thus, in the Western world, the religious crusade for democratic reform in the seventeenth and eighteenth centuries was not generated in the all-encompassing homeland of the Catholic Church, but in the Spartan exclusiveness of Calvinism, especially in the left-wing Puritan sects. In America during the same period, the most radical political communities, by anyone's measurement, were the Puritan "Kingdoms of God" that settled on the Eastern seaboard and that proceeded to equate their own "sense of the meeting" with the will of God. More recently, the demands for civil and racial justice did not grow out of the eclectic middle class, with its radical experimentalism. From the earliest days of the Montgomery bus boycott and the freedom rides, the movement was made up of the pure in heart, who could enjoy the winds of political significance on their faces because they were utterly convinced about the rightness of their cause. The self-sacrifice needed to make protest movements flourish is seldom found in the radical middle class. It is the fruit of clarity and consistency, and the more sophistic temper of suburbia does not seem to be able to produce this important precondition.

In his book *One-Dimensional Man,* Herbert Marcuse goes a step farther in his description of how the pluralistic industrial culture represses protest by legitimating and therefore defusing it. Not only does the culture protect itself with its protean style, it encourages an understanding of logic—the normative pattern of political argument—that makes protest unlikely. For persons who have missed the luxury of a college major in philosophy, Marcuse's argument here is both obscure and demanding, but his point is directly aimed at what we have called suburban sophistry. The suburban sophist, the radical, in his politics betrays an intellectual habit that Marcuse sees as the devastating culmination of Western man's refusal to deal prophetically with himself and his culture. The pattern of reasoning, the logic, is the philosophical analogue to the institutional arrangements that have sustained one-dimensional culture.[30]

Under the spell of the linguistic-analytic revolution in philosophy, Marcuse says, Western man has given up the hope of finding political truth, and he is no longer interested in inquiring about the validity or invalidity of political arguments. Instead, he is willing to believe that different arguments have their own standards of measurement, their own inherent logics. All that is asked is that persons play according to the rules, with whatever perspectives they happen to have chosen. In other words, Western man has learned to live with logics, and does not believe that he has at his disposal an instrument (logical criticism) that allows him to transcend various political arguments and to make judgments about them. Competitive political perspectives thus are granted relative autonomy. They are seen to be self-contained "language games," which do not contact each other within a process of mutual criticism that has some prospect of resolution.

According to Marcuse, linguistic analysis' contentment to explore a pluralism of logics is "academic sado-masochism, self-humiliation, and self-denunciation." As an assumption about the way political arguments should be measured, however, the pluralistic approach is disastrous for the function of social prophecy. It does not encourage people to question whether "ordinary language" about politics is profitable or validly developed, and it does not create the impetus to forge beyond a culture's political common sense to a higher level of insight.[31]

It is hardly surprising that, reared in the ethos that gave birth to the linguistic revolution in philosophy, the scientifically oriented, affluent Western man should also develop a social character that leaves everything politically as it is. In an important sense, the expansive character appears as a fleshly realization of the linguistic revolution—one that holds a kind of reverence for alternative ways of experiencing the world and, also, alternative frames of reference for arguing about the "good society." The style is sophistic, just as the linguistic-analytic preoccupation with logics must be understood as an expression of the sophistic spirit.

The Politics of Healing

Our experience with middle-class sophistry tends to confirm Marcuse's observation that pluralistic reason, the respect for a variety of logics, may contribute to the defeat of effective protest. We have noticed over and over that the

radicality of the American suburb looks like a conservative political movement, in spite of the fact that expansive
persons often cannot believe that their liberated, experimental behavior is supportive of the political *status quo*.
The conservative tendencies of the radical suburb, however, are not ideological. Expansive persons do not hew
out of stone a creed in order to oppose the theoretical
foundations of protest politics. Their conservatism is more
by default—the absence of interest in consistent political
involvement, the absence of discipline, the reaction against
tightness in any form.

Strangely, it is precisely this absence of ideological identity that makes sophist styles so potentially useful and positive in American politics at this particular time and in this
particular climate, even though it would be bizarre to imagine a totally expansive political game. American politics
are presently suffering from a severe congestion. The channels of nourishment and of release seem blocked, and
breathing is too hard. In the latter part of the 1960's,
millions of conscientious and savage Americans moved
into positions of perpetual opposition, opposing the "others," whom they knew through the press and television.
They continue to glare at each other, and steadfast loyalties
bind people together in quasi-military formations. It is all
reminiscent of the long, sedentary war in Virginia, with the
Army of the Potomac frightened, holding to camp, and
now and then roaming outward to meet the Army of North-
ern Virginia—to stumble into infernal battles where American youths dispatched each other to Christianity's heaven,
only to hurry back to camp in order to glower toward
Richmond and recoup for the next killing. Whites against
blacks, young against old, rural areas against the metropolis, suburbs against downtowns: they all seem to be in the
process of encamping, pulling together to cut off peaceful
communication.

In this situation, where political polarization appears to

be a major barrier to both civil peace and urban innovation, there is something to be said for the maverick, sophist style of leadership where clarity and consistency diminish in value. The maverick—the new sophist—generally has a political history that is best described as a series of happenings, not the evolution of a political philosophy. He often looks slippery and devoid of sincere conviction. He is more interesting than profound, more entertaining than inspiring, and more likely to be someone you would not want your daughter to marry. He often surrounds himself with political advisers who are indistinguishable from advertising executives, and he is able to project a number of conflicting images simultaneously.

In Los Angeles, for example, the expansive mayor manages to play the embattled opponent of the goliath city newspaper, the defender of industry interests, the champion of the average citizen, the one who exposes the absenteeism of city councilmen, the one who is himself often absent from the city doing good works, the defender of local control, and the maker of the city's foreign policy. He is a man for all seasons, at every moment, and few in the great metropolis are bored by his antics. He is not a hero, by any means, but he makes for a fascinating evening of story-swapping. When you mention his name, several persons will instinctively wince, but the resultant conversation can make the dullest party into a vast success.

Another political figure surrounds himself with an incongruous group of advisers whose political complexions include almost every point of the spectrum. He administers a circus, where the schedule of events makes no sense at all except as a way to keep the spectators guessing. Just when you think he agrees with you, he does something remarkably out of joint. No one can identify with him completely. But then no one can feel totally alienated either.

The politics of sophistry demand verve, showmanship, and often a large supply of fortitude. Yet they are not calculated to encourage confidence among social protesters. Sophist politicians are not likely to inspire the kind of loyalty that will make schoolchildren want to collect pennies to erect bronze memorials. When crowds gather at the airport to greet a sophist politician, a goodly percentage may think of Senator Foghorn from Li'l Abner's home district. The politics of sophistry can be healing, though, in spite of the fact that their fickleness also can enrage reformers and revolutionaries. They can keep everybody off guard in a period when citizens are tense with each other and when to have a clearly defined leader is to damage the identification of larger numbers of persons with their ship of state. Periods of sophist leadership are not exactly periods of inactivity, because presumably what needs to be accomplished is the preservation of at least a minimally stable society. Likewise, periods of sophist leadership are not exactly preservers of the civic *status quo,* because in the course of the expansive circus, remarkable innovations can be accomplished.

As we have observed earlier, the expansive style is ideally suited to peaceful times, so when the citizenry is highly polarized, the sophist has a vested interest in relieving tensions. In fact, he may be the one most likely to succeed in effecting the reforms needed to establish a more just and therefore less violent society. Ideologues, however realistic their politics might be, are likely to inspire division, where compromise is unlikely. Or they can splinter their society into competitive savage tribes, where political battles are fought out in the spirit of holy wars. In contrast, the maverick is able to announce plans that are astonishingly progressive. But he can avoid the holocaust because he has already paid his obeisance to rightist commitments. At least in token ways, he has established his credentials in a number of political traditions. Periods of sophist leadership, therefore, do not produce the wholesale reform desired by many, and certainly not the quantity of legislation engineered by Franklin Roosevelt in his presidential honeymoon. Yet the maverick, if he is doing his job, may accomplish much that needs to be done without risking revolution and, if he is lucky, without furthering the conditions that lead in that direction. "Loose" is what redeeming politics must be; and, if nothing else, sophistry is loose.

Of course, the sophist style of politics is not self-sufficient, and it alone cannot be depended upon to deliver Americans from their period of civic turmoil. Gadflies are interesting and often productive, but they seldom are able to build the climate in which reform becomes politically expedient. The illness of polarized politics grows from the illness of problems left unsolved and injustices ignored. And the sophist becomes exciting only as both forms of illness are treated. Expansive politicians can succeed in finding solutions, yet they need the activity of conscientious community organizers—strikers, picketers, organizers of boycotts. Without their work, the sophist politics of healing can turn into a merry-go-round of interesting events, all of which serve the purposes of the sophist himself, and all of which easily promote a disgusting form of demagoguery.

The Politics of Imagination

What looks like a loss of faith within persons who do not worry about political consistency may well be the prelude to a very creative political transformation in the West. There is little question that the neat separation of ideologies into conservative and liberal (with right wing and far left at the extremes) is coming to an end, mainly because of a lack of imagination. Arguments about property rights, capital punishment, the role of government, the right of society to seek its own collective welfare, and on and on, were developed with depth and complexity in the latter days of the nineteenth century, but the lines of argument have hardly changed since then. Political debate has become routine, quite predictable, and—except for issues that touch immediate interests—not very stimulating. If anything, debate was better in the nineteenth century before ideas became slogans.

More distressing is the fact that many issues on the agenda in the latter part of this century resist being handled on the rightist-leftist scale. One thinks, for example, of the rather universal disillusionment with the possibilities provided by the large federal bureaucracy in handling metropolitan and rural ills, and, also, the broad-scale reaction against the national welfare structure. These cannot be viewed as victories for either liberals or conservatives, and the directions for change can hardly be mapped in the familiar ways. Robert Kennedy saw this fact in the presidential primaries of 1968, and, at least in California, he had almost everyone simultaneously elated, angered, and confused. To some, he sounded like a red-neck, while to others he sounded like a rank socialist. To still others, he appeared simply to be playing dirty pool in a state where he had to win decisively. Informed opinion, though, recognized that Kennedy was the prophet of twentieth-century discontent with the political wisdom of the nineteenth century. He had not developed a clear alternative, but at least he was aware of the problem.

In California, Kennedy showed possibilities for blossoming into a fully developed sophist. He was casting around for arguments that might or might not fit, all in the hope of finding a healing, experimental direction for the new politics. His death in Los Angeles was a tragedy for the politics of imagination, because he was the only celebrated sophist at work in the camp of individuals who had been reared as liberals. For the moment, the sophist initiative was given, by default, to leadership whose ideological roots were in the conservative territory of Whittier. Sophists have a propensity, when they are overwhelmed by the pressures of office or campaigning, to fall back on their former doctrinal rigidities. So it is healthy to have sophists with various origins working out their futures on the American scene. There is need for a credentialed liberal to assume the sophist mantle of Robert Kennedy.

Two key happenings in suburbia signal a disengagement from the liberal-conservative frame of reference for political debate and provide encouragement for the formulation of a sophist style that is more germane to current issues:

1. The jarring intrusion of concern about the quality of American life into political dialogue. Liberal-conservative politics are concerned with quantity, not quality. Debates have to do with adding and subtracting rights and privileges, reallocating resources, providing services, distributing burdens and benefits—all of which can be summarized neatly in the annual budget. The matter of quality has carefully been avoided, largely because it seems divorced from what can be accomplished in the legislative chambers, and also because it confuses political questions with religious or philosophical convictions. What politicians actually can do about the quality of American life, other than rejuggle the budget and organize a few agencies, is problematic. They can talk about it; charismatic leadership can affect national ethos; and imaginative programs can assure citizens about national purposes. But, to say the least, a political process that is asked to deal with "the decline of values" or "depersonalization" is a process that is in trouble.

The effect, however, is therapeutic. Like the playful revolution of the hippie subculture, described by Herbert Marcuse, the words and issues assault the very categories in which politics proceed. Blaming political institutions for the quality of culture, the citizen makes business-as-usual appear to be anachronistic, out of touch with issues that really matter. The frame of reference itself becomes an issue, and people start talking about the "old politics," as if talking about their death will make them die. The fact that this curious concern with quality seems to be growing rather than disappearing indicates a period of ideological loosening up, where the premium is placed on imagination, and where alternative frames of political preference have some chance of gaining vitality.

2. A second happening is the stylistic realignment of suburban politics, a phenomenon we have already mentioned. Suburbanites are dividing themselves into zealots and gradualists, and whatever the matter at hand, a feeling grows that the larger issue concerns which style will predominate. A recent conversation with a so-called urban revolutionary, for example, revealed the surprising fact that he counted the Ku Klux Klan, the John Birch Society, and similar organizations to be among his closest allies, all of whom were working to deliver middle-class America from its one-dimensional malaise. The problem, he said, was to get the issues straight and to create situations where citizens can intelligently make clear-cut choices. He saw himself as the representative of a zealot community doing the spadework necessary for the coming battle among belief systems.

In contrast, many suburbanites believe that gradualism ought to be defended, because it is the only style that can keep a multifactional society from tribal war. By their lights, the threat of the urban revolutionary is his temperament and his tightness, not particularly his policies (with which they might even agree).

The stylistic division, however, takes attention away from routine categories of political commentary and thus becomes potentially useful. The possibility of interesting, new alliances is created. A space to imagine alternative approaches is guarded. And, although we cannot project what will finally emerge, it is possible to imagine a disengagement from the right-left definition of choices. The preoccupation with style assaults the main-line tradition of Western political philosophy, in spite of the fact that pragmatism has always had its philosophical defenders. The offense is in the possibility that stylistic politics are self-consciously destructive of ends that even pragmatism in America has perennially served.

The politics of sophistry may or may not be shaping a viable, imaginative alternative to liberalism and conservatism. It is too early to know; and it is certainly too early to become excited about the birth of a new political idea. The times do seem to be right, however, to affirm maverick, sophist styles as a helpful presence, and to counter the idea that sophist moves are always insincere moves. At least we can say that sophistry provides an opening up, where healing can progress and, hopefully, where imagination can be stimulated.

Chapter 8

SUBURBAN RADICALITY:
A NEW NIHILISM?

FOR MANY middle-class Americans, 1964 was a year they would rather forget. That was the year, of course, that Berkeley's free speech movement challenged business-as-usual in the administration of higher education, and set into motion a series of student protests that moved dizzily between the absurd and the lofty, the playful and the tensely revolutionary. As almost any resident of Berkeley knows, the drama was quickly exaggerated out of all proportion to what occurred. Especially within the mentality of suburban savagery, the free speech movement appeared to be a horrendous climax to the postwar assault on American unity, more poisonous even than the Communist conspiracy or the civil rights movement, because it was a crusade of, by, and for offspring of the middle class—a festering from within the ranks. Correctly or mistakenly, then, 1964 became the year when many middle-class citizens began to have the terrible fear that here, in the very heartland of affluent security, a nihilistic younger generation had been fathered.

But Berkeley's student protest was not in itself a turning point, only the occasion for a newsworthy dramatization of long-established nihilist trends in middle-class America. Since at least World War II, for example, suburban intellectuals had been drinking at the fount of Jean-Paul Sartre and others of his ilk, persons who had lost faith in the vision of universal truth and moral law, and who shared a deep sense of the purposelessness of human existence. Ironically, the so-called "complacent 1950's" granted economic support to Europe's Theater of the Absurd, and turned *Death of a Salesman*'s despairing Willy Loman into a folk hero who had to be reckoned with by virtually every moralizer in the nation. In the 1950's, also, the existentialist literary tradition was rediscovered and popularized by Christian theologians. And with its faddish utilization in middle-class discussion groups came all sorts of anti-institutional biases, doubts about the value of belief systems, and suspicions about the arbitrariness of moral convictions. Thus, even while middle-class Americans were demonstrating their complacency with the adequacy of the suburban utopia, and even while they were crowding into churches to celebrate the religious foundations of their shared dreams, there were telltale signs of nihilism. Nihilism could no longer be regarded as the private burden of a czarist Russia or of a politically unstable France; it was as American as Yankee-Doodle.

What about the coming of expansive man, though? Does he represent a culmination of this nihilistic rejection of moral order, truth, purpose, and the validity of traditional institutions? Is this the way the Age of Moral Man ends in the West—not with a bang, but with the giggles of expansive man swimming in a suburban pool? Does expansive man initiate a new age where sin has no meaning and where moral failure is no longer a serious possibility?

Expansiveness and Moral Decline

Much of what people see as moral decline within the radical middle class is really irrationalism—a lack of inter-

est in integrating lives around coherent sets of moral principles, a lack of interest in systematically justifying life-
styles in philosophical terms, and a discovery of virtue in
the vital, emotive dimension of man's constitution. And, as
we have already observed, this irrationalism has long been
a mark of the American character, variously interpreted as
frontier pragmatism or as the ever-present possibility of
emotional, anti-intellectual mass movements. If irrationalism constitutes moral disintegration, expansive man is
merely the victim of a peculiarly American brand of original sin. He should not be saddled with the unjust accusa-
tion that he is doing anything very unique in his experimentalism with sin.

The relatively new factor in the situation, though, has to
do with guilt. And at this point, grounds can more legitimately be found for uneasiness about the moral health of
radicality. It is not simply that expansive man disagrees
with traditional beliefs about what is good, right, and oblig-
atory. Westerners are accustomed by now to arguments on
this level, and have learned to live with the fact that different moral ideals compete with one another for public
attention. Rather, uneasiness is generated by the fact that
guilt seems to be a dying emotion, and that the moral liberation in America seems to be a liberation from norms
themselves. The new situation, whose lines are only now
taking shape, can give the impression that expansive individuals are creating a moral environment that minimizes
the ascetic ideals that have plagued and inspired conscientious individuals for the past twenty-five hundred years.

Probably the most carefully developed, as well as the
most provocative, account of this impression is Philip
Rieff's *The Triumph of the Therapeutic*. Rieff argues that
the affluent American is experiencing a "feeling of symbolic impoverishment," wherein traditionally powerful
ideals are losing their ability to elicit an intense interest.
"Even the religiously inclined grow more diffuse in their

self-demand, praising 'faith in life,' " he writes. "And those without even this general faith . . . are hailed as most religious because they can find nothing to obey or await." [32] Rieff, in fact, sees a cultural revolution in process—one that moves far beyond that which Max Weber called "disenchantment" toward decay of the classical Western systems of moral demand, religious and philosophical. The movement is in the direction of release, toward a therapeutic ideal, where the image of fulfilled personhood is that of a "needy person, permanently engaged in the task of achieving a gorgeous variety of satisfactions." [33] The revolution is anticreedal, witnessing the end of religious and political man within Western history.

In sociological terms, Rieff describes the situation as one where release mechanisms are assuming a heightened importance. Every culture, he says, has two essential functions: (1) the maintenance and enforcement of a system of moral demands and (2) the organization of means by which persons can find release, to some extent, from the strain of these demands. At various times in a culture's history, one of these functions will tend to predominate, and the whole tenor of that culture's moral climate will be determined by what is occurring in that tenuous and shifting balance of controls and releases.[34] In our own period, we are experiencing a moral revolution precisely because the releasing, permissive mechanisms are more compelling than the controlling ones, or, at least, the releasing mechanisms are so nearly equal to controls in their force that neither can assert social authority.[35]

Rieff claims that in all cultures before our own, periods of heightened release made fertile ground for the growth of new systems of control—beliefs and values that did have the power to excite and to provide a frame of reference wherein a culture could experience moral consensus. But conditions appear to be different now. No alternative system of control is achieving social force; the cultural revolution is "deliberately not in the name of any new order of communal purpose." [36] It has not produced a moral elite, whose function would be to surround new controls with a justifying atmosphere, and it has not (in fact, it could not) produce communities, associations, or institutions, where shared rituals and symbols serve to enforce the new forms of moral command. The cultural revolution, Rieff says, is antinormative, antipolitical, anticommunal—a state of affairs which, from any perspective, would have to be interpreted as profoundly nihilistic. The affluent suburbanite loses the occasion for agonizing about his sin, because sin depends upon systems of ideals that define what moral failure is. Guilt belongs to the pretherapeutic era.

Rieff's hypothesis deserves to be taken seriously. It is brilliant. But we will have to conclude finally that his apocalyptic announcement concerning the death of moral norms, and therefore the demise of guilt, is premature. Rieff's strength is his ability to account for expansive styles in terms of Freudian social theory, yet his Freudian biases also make it difficult for him to see what there is to see in the American suburb. Of course, no one can look at moral change in an objective way, since observation is always selective and is always affected by a person's world view. Rieff is no exception, nor are we. And we are not uneasy with *The Triumph of the Therapeutic* just because it is so blatant a production of the Freudian camp. Our criticism is that it does not handle the data of middle-class behavior in an adequate way, and even ignores whole dimensions of the suburban scene.

Rieff's view that the cultural revolution is nihilistic rests on some surprising assumptions. The only norms about which he will speak, for example, are principles that command renunciation. Norms are ascetic by definition and grow out of faith communities, such as churches, which place a high value on sacrifice, because ethical-religious communities have traditionally had to minister within an economy of scarcity. So when Rieff pictures the man who embodies Western moral and religious styles, he sees a sufferer who is trying to find ways of making self-deprivation more palatable. From his point of view, then, to be set free from the need to accept economic deprivation is to be released from the need for guilt and the need for community. In a society such as ours where abundance rather than scarcity is the rule, the social utility of guilt is eased, and the reason for spawning systems of sacrificial demand disappears. Abundance spells the end of moral law because the projection of norms is a response to hard economic reality. As Rieff says, the rich no longer require so stern a superego.

Rieff's assumptions do not allow him to see that the expansive suburbanite who flits from one interesting experience to another really has not been delivered from guilt, from the irritating, sometimes devastating sense of moral failure, or even from the intuition that life is to be lived within a moral order. Rieff gives us a cartoon. Ascetic, sacrificially oriented norms are not the only kind to be found under the sun. And although affluence may rob certain images of the good life of their power, it does not automatically usher in a new nihilist age. The suburban radical has suffered a moral loss, because the principles, ideals, and models that inspire his savage and conscientious neighbors do not usually excite him. But he is not profligate. It is this fact which needs exploration here.

The Radical as Assemblage Artist

H. Richard Niebuhr's posthumous volume, *The Responsible Self*,[37] seems particularly germane in finding a way of looking at the morals of expansive man. Niebuhr, following Ernst Cassirer, argues that man is first and foremost a symbol maker: he uses images, words, and marks as well

as highly abstract signs in the development of his thought;
he is artistically creative in articulating feelings; and he
produces myths to formulate intuitions about his physical
and social universe. In turn, Niebuhr says, the symbols
have a power of their own, once they are born. Although
the symbols are products of human intelligence, they also
affect the way persons think about themselves. That is,
they shape the identity of persons.

Niebuhr illustrates his broad point by looking at what
people are actually doing when they try to picture the process of "being moral." He shows that persons tend to take
symbols—especially images—and make these into models
of morality. For example, many Westerners have used the
image of man as a builder: an engineer with a blueprint in
mind, the task being to take the resources at hand in order
to implement that blueprint. So it is with the moral life:
the symbol shapes the moral style as morality comes to be
seen as the process of life-building. Persons may disagree
with one another about what the ideal finished product
should be, but they agree that being moral is implementing
a blueprint, or an image of the good life, whether that be
a life of pleasure, a life that emulates the habits of Jesus,
or a life that is dedicated to being rational.[38]

Other persons, Niebuhr says, habitually think of "being
moral" as a process of living obediently under the moral
law. Their formative symbol is the image of man as a citizen, or man as a child who is disciplined by authoritarian
parents. Living the moral life has to do with duty and dis-
cerning obligation, and it is more concerned with following
the law than with calculating distant, future consequences.
Such persons tend toward legalism, both temperamental
and intellectual. They will try mightily to make their concrete moral choices to be consistent with the broad laws,
which appear to be authoritative.[39]

Translating Rieff's case concerning symbolic impoverishment into Niebuhrian terms, it is certainly the case that

symbolic forms can gain and lose the power to shape a culture's consensus about what is morally appropriate. Such symbols are products of the human intelligence and are not written in the stars. Certain symbols may indeed assume tremendous moral authority at those times when they are widely assumed within a culture. But symbols, like man himself, are historically rooted and subject to change. To believe that the loss of certain symbols, or even the loss of a whole genre of symbols, is tantatmount to nihilism is little short of blatant symbolic idolatry.

It is a wholesome fact that in the Western tradition, and more particularly the Judeo-Christian tradition, no one symbol has been deified as the definitive image of "being moral." In the New Testament, for example, the good life is pictured in any number of ways. Christians are urged to be disciples of Christ, to be imitators of Christ, to be subject to the law, to be free from the law, to live in the Spirit, to walk in the light, to be peacemakers, to be bearers of the sword of righteousness, to be crucified. If one goes to the trouble of sorting out which writers use which symbols, it can be shown that some writers are fairly consistent in their symbols, but others, such as the apostle Paul, seem to care not a whit for consistency. Symbols are not to be made into idols.

Affluent individuals find it increasingly difficult to get very excited about living their lives like engineers (because they are not sure that an adequate blueprint is available), or like citizens under the law (because laws have too often been discredited as instruments of injustice). But their lives are not necessarily nihilistic. It may simply be that other symbols are finding new energy in the suburbs and that other forms of moral identity are becoming more satisfying bases for cultural consensus, at least among the radical minority.

But what are the symbols around which expansive suburbanites are forming their moral behavior? If, as we are arguing, suburban radicality is not a release from norms, what are its norms?

Constitutive symbols can be discovered only inductively. They are never on the surface, because they provide the fundamental patterns in which thinking proceeds. Few conscientious suburbanites would say, for example, "Being moral is like being an engineer," or "Being moral is like living under the law." The symbols are present and are effective in forming moral styles. Still, they are hidden. They are the medium rather than the substance of arguments about what is good, bad, just, and unjust. Probably the best way to recognize constitutive symbols is to listen carefully to what words are repeatedly used, what kinds of illustrations are applied, how disagreements are settled, and, if possible, what kinds of things are not talked about. These can become clues by which configurations of moral reasoning are illumined and the character of effective norms understood.

In our case, the clues suggest that the suburbs are producing moral styles appropriate to the image of man as an artist. The words that describe the suburban radical are words that apply to the artistic endeavor as well as to radical suburban living: process, technique, creativity, style, imagination, sensuality, aesthetic satisfaction. They have to do with finding value in a process that resists the mechanical application of principles or laws, which is not content with projecting blueprints for the good life, but which is uneasy with the proposal that there are no norms whatsoever. The artistic process gives birth to its own standards of order, and so can be interpreted as an alternative experience of moral command.

The artistic model which informs the radical suburban ethic can be viewed in terms of the process by which junk art or assemblage art is created—objects fashioned out of materials collected from drawers, attics, garages, vacant lots, junkyards, and city dumps. Assemblage art may not particularly be the crowning achievement of twentieth-century creativity, but it is an expression of urban and suburban life. It is fashioned out of things that are liberally available in the suburb; the components are bits and pieces of a familiar environment, aspects of the artist's immediate experience.

In making an assemblage art object, the artist welds or wires together an assortment of incongruous articles. One of us, for example, recently constructed an assemblage sculpture out of nursery (shrub) cans, the iron support for a laundry tub, a wrought-iron fixture, toy beads, assorted tin-can lids, a drawer pull, a container originally filled with barbecue lighter fluid, and a number of metal washers. In their origins, of course, the articles were unrelated, but the fun of being an assemblage artist is in bringing a kind of integrity to diversity—especially if the various pieces of junk are never altered from the condition in which they were discovered.

The surprising thing in the process, though, is that not just anything will do. When the arrangement of component parts attempts to be profound in its social commentary (like the elaborate war machines exhibited in countless art festivals) or elegant in its beauty, a violation of the form has occurred. Assemblage art is playful. Like other varieties of pop art, it attempts to redeem the commonplace through mock reverence—a spirit that nonetheless heightens awareness of the beauty of the manufactured environment. This redemption always occurs in the classic spirit of comedy, with the same commitment as the clown, who honors common human emotions by exaggerating them and dealing with them in a context of play. For all its grossness, assemblage art, to be successful, must adhere strictly to the canons of stylistic appropriateness. It can be a terrible art form, a coarse satire on the artistic process itself. But rightly conceived and executed, it blossoms into a form that is happily at home as suburban folk art.

We would not care to suggest that making assemblage art constitutes a model for the moral life of the radical suburb, or that the underlying patterns of expansiveness can be determined by close analogy. That would be a strained attempt, somewhat comical in itself. We are suggesting, though, that the comparison is helpful in allowing us to recognize the lines of expansive ethics, particularly in showing that aesthetically oriented expansiveness is a thoroughly normative alternative. Like the assemblage artist, the suburban radical is a partisan. He is not morally neutral, dabbling in experiences while being oblivious to the demands of moral order. Like the assemblage artist, the radical is working out a model of moral behavior that contains the possibility of violation and that contends for an ordered form of moral existence.

The norms of this model are less propositional than they are aesthetic. They are like the requirements experienced within a process where one attempts to find a sense of fulfillment, rightness, and equilibrium. When the assemblage artist, for example, finds a piece that is crudely placed, he knows that his sculpture is not right and he will work until the proper location and the appropriate anchorage are discovered. The artist finds it virtually impossible to describe, in terms of rules, the difference between the shoddy and the satisfying object, but he knows himself to be under demands that cannot be ignored if he is to maintain respect for his own integrity. The difference between the two states of completion is recognizable, but the variable is the practiced hand of the artist.

The reason that expansiveness appears so close to nihilism is that the norms of aesthetic moral equilibrium are so difficult to translate into propositions, and, in fact, they become something other than themselves in the attempt. Artists have not been delivered from norms, but nonartists persist in thinking that anything goes in modern art and that a few thoughtless strokes of the brush are all that is needed to turn out an acceptable art object. Artists are usually inadequate, however, in their apology for their professional moral commitments. In a sense, one must experience the process to know its burdens. And one must feel guilty about his inability to complete a satisfying object before he can be convinced that there is such a thing as aesthetic failure.

Determining his life-styles in terms of an image of the artist at work, the radical, also, may uncover his constitutive symbols in his own disturbing experience of failure and guilt.

Expansive personalities know that they have failed when, through weakness, ignorance, or self-centering panic, they fail to be open to their surroundings, to persons, beliefs, and life possibilities. Sin is being closed, being static, not recognizing what there is to see, being blind, not affirming the worth of the physical. The radical life, then, is affirmative, and failure arises out of forces, both personal and social, that serve to kill interests and to turn people in upon themselves.

Conscientiousness stands as an attractive temptation, because it offers the gift of social and intellectual security and also the possibility of an integrated world view. But it is a temptation to be resisted. Conscientiousness is restrictive, and leads to the division of world views into those which are acceptable and those which are not. It places certain experiences outside the pale and thus represents a failure—the failure to know the finiteness of symbolic inventions. Suburban savagery likewise provides a viable way of experiencing the world, at least in limited circumstances, yet it too must be counted as an expansive sin in its nervous defense of tribal mores. Savagery counts as idolatry, in the degree to which it makes competitive world views and life possibilities into enemies to be annihilated.

Expansive social sin has to do with closedness also, but mainly with the ways in which communities foreclose possibilities, abhor gadflies, and do not allow persons to work out their own salvation with verve and eclectic radicality. In other words, social sin is the failure to encourage the morally artistic process. Expansiveness requires a universal commitment to nurturing the conditions within which imagination is not damned, oddity is not confused with insanity, and playfulness is not mistaken for a lack of seriousness.

But the greatest of all social-political sins is poverty—the money kind. Moral artistry requires moral paintbrushes: the leisure, the equipment, and the social mobility necessary to play the radical game. If the philosopher Immanuel Kant is correct in maintaining that there is something terribly immoral about making an exception of oneself in the face of ethical obligation, the suburban radical must accept the "imperative of affluence." That is, as he enjoys the expansive style, he ought to realize that the style needs affluence; and he surely must know that to affirm the radical concept of man is broadly to affirm its economic foundations. His social responsibility is to extend affluence, to bring people into the middle class where they can be free, and to bury the distorting stereotypes about happy peasants, coercive affluent societies, and regressive middle-class institutions.

When expansive man happily works out his own radical salvation without reference to the relative economic isolation of his class, he fails morally. Welfare reform, the extension of Social Security, the availability of medical services, fair-employment practices, and regional economic planning ought to be endemic to the radical position, because without these, the radical perpetuates his isolation from large portions of his own society. Tragically, he also creates the social unrest and tension that encourage suburban and urban savagery and hinder his own mobility. The failure is not best interpreted as a lapse in liberal commitments. To ignore the imperative of affluence is a sin against that expansiveness which the radical believes to be a step forward in man's faltering progress toward creating more humane and exciting forms of human existence.

The stylistic community of expansive man is ideally universal. It cannot, with good reason, exclude persons along arbitrary lines, because finally the implicit ideal is an inclusive society of sharply defined, beautiful people, who are held together because they are interesting to one another and because they affirm one another's right to experimentalism. In the less-than-perfect world, of course, few of us are either strikingly interesting or beautiful, and the community of the radical suburb can be experienced as exclusive and stylistically dogmatic. In the presence of the beautiful people, the radical elite, we often feel out of place—even overwhelmed. Yet the ideal, the vision of a heavenly, radical city, is one where the potential of Everyman is appreciated and the eclectic, playful style is endowed with self-confidence. The vision is far from being nihilistic or anarchical. It constitutes instead the projection of an ideal that is consistent with the kinds of social relatedness encouraged by the affluent, scientific era.

Radicality and Transcendence

The most frightening specter of nihilism, though, arises out of fears that the new middle-class ideal locks persons into a never-ending now, a merry-go-round of happenings wherein there are few occasions for considering the larger issues of moral well-being. In brief, it can be claimed that the radical lacks a long view—perspective. He loses interest in self-transcendence; and, far more seriously in the eyes of some, he is in danger of losing the ability to find reminders of a transcendent God in his makeshift, experimental world.

These fears grow from the obvious pathologies of middle-class America, particularly the interminable identity crises and the suburb's grotesque inability to deal with the problem of death. H. Richard Niebuhr accurately reflects these fears in his description of persons who cannot say which part of themselves is the Real Self—persons who cannot find a sense of wholeness within their experience of conflicting loyalties and beliefs. The suspicion inevitably grows that the American situation encourages a spirit of resignation to dividedness and cannot supply the compensating experience of fulfillment—a feeling of satisfaction with the dignity of intraself pluralism. It does not help, Niebuhr says, to be told that the unity of man is achieved in the awareness that he, divided wretch that he is, will die all at one time.[40]

This image of the suburbanite who cannot achieve self-transcendence, though, rests upon a misunderstanding of what is happening in middle-class America. If anything, the radical suburbanite asserts with a vengeance his ability to be master of his own merry-go-round. To change the metaphor, he asserts his right to the self-transcendence of the artist, who does not lose perspective in the process of playing with rock, paint, and canvas. The artist is a craftsman only as he succeeds in rising above the childish propensity to experiment thoughtlessly. And so it is with suburban radicality: the very mark of its character is self-transcendence, the ability to choose and designedly to weave together fragments from an array of perspectives and behavioral possibilities.

In the Judeo-Christian West, an uneasiness could also be felt with suburbia's apparent loss of taste for divine grace, or what Protestants know as justification by faith. This is the intuition that man cannot forever be his own master, and that moral uplift must depend on an act of divine forgiveness, a being grasped and energized from outside.

There are signs, however, that suburban radicals, with their religious and quasi-religious fads, have not even lost this taste, nor the intuition of divine grace. What is new is the startling pluralism of symbols and experiences that direct attention to the mystery of being and that provide for the conceptualization of the depth and source of being. If expansive man's alchemy and Christ, astrology and scientism, and rationalism and mysticism appear crude, at least the style reflects a healthy suspicion of symbols. The radical believes that when symbols are taken too seriously, they cease to be pointers to realities beyond themselves and become barriers—idols that foreclose further insight. Playfulness and eclecticism express his unashamed acceptance of man's location in history, with all that this location means by way of depriving him of omniscience. Caught in history, radical man celebrates the lack of connectedness of his religious experiences and symbols, because this very absence of order reminds him that he cannot readily put his finger on the universal pulse. Paradoxically, dividedness can become for him the vehicle by which he points to the God of the Judeo-Christian faith, whose oneness and whose sovereignty stand in contrast to man's eclectic attempts to penetrate mystery symbolically.

Expansive eclecticism can also be a way of affirming that the God of the Judeo-Christian tradition is at work throughout his creation. The tradition, in its finest expression, has never tried to limit the activity of God entirely to the confines of the organizational church, nor has it believed that formal doctrinal systems provide the exhaustive statement about man's relation to the divine. Balking at the thought that there is but one approach to perceiving the transcendent, the most creative theologians have drawn extensively on the work of a number of intellectual disciplines, and have even run the risk of losing the identity of theology in the potpourri. Consequently, expansiveness hardly seems to be heresy. Expansive saints affirm their openness to the divine in the multiplicity of their perspectives, and they tend to demonstrate a beautifully serious sensitivity to what is there in creation to be appreciated.

Creation, they know, has an integrity of its own, to be enjoyed for its own sake. But things and objects and events can be experienced in different ways—including ways that grant access to the being grasped by mystery.

Philosophical and religious thinkers have always learned from less reflective neighbors, and they usually have not been reticent to accept their leadership. Defensiveness is a peril, as is prematurely making negative judgments about jarring cultural styles. In the current situation, these perils seem great, because Westerners believe they are losing traditional forms of faith and the middle class seems so intent on cutting itself loose from familiar symbols of the past. So traditionalists feel threatened.

That is unfortunate, because when people become tense they sometimes lose the ability to affirm emergent possibilities. The radical suburb, to be explicit, seems to offer fresh possibilities for being human, and we ought not to miss the opportunity to evaluate ourselves and our culture in its terms. Threats have a way of turning into delights, and we believe that such will increasingly be the case with the radical suburb.

Part II

———————

**SOUNDINGS
IN EXPANSIVE CHARACTER**

INTRODUCTORY COMMENTS

THIS IS A COLLECTION of "soundings"—intended as an invitation to cooperative exploration into this business of radicality in the suburbs. The explorations (which readers can easily multiply) are intended to be suggestive rather than determinative; useful rather than definitive. They fall somewhere between the abstractness of the ideal types we have just developed and the intimate concreteness of personal experience; and they are designed to trigger a progressive awareness of expansive man's presence. By offering a few diverse case studies in suburban radicality, we mean to encourage readers to go on to their own soundings, to see expansiveness everywhere. Our soundings, however, are not determinative, because our hypothesis is not determinative in the common sense of the word. To set out a picture of expansive man is somewhat like eliciting the traditional picture of Renaissance Man: scholars have known for a long time that rigorous historical studies will turn up no one Renaissance Man. Indeed, studies of the Renaissance show that (as in any age) the human landscape was extremely varied. Nonetheless, scholars do not casually reject the suggestive image of Renaissance Man. Together, as a whole, men of the period were definitely caught up in a spirit and a task that can be distinguished from, say, the Medieval spirit and task.[41] The stylistic concept of Renaissance Man does mean something; it has (and had for men of the Renaissance in an embryonic way) a functional and interpretative meaning. Through its suggestiveness, men of the fourteenth century knew themselves, and through it we know them. But ideal types are not universal or generic concepts that determine the nature of particulars within the genus. We know, for example, that it is meaningful to talk about American character or Mexican character, Buddhist mentality or Christian mentality, without having to say that every American, Mexican, Buddhist, or Christian does act in such and such a way, or even that any one of these individuals fulfills the qualities of our characterization.

Ideal types are "group concepts." Group concepts are not statements about individual psychology or subjective phenomenology. They suggest instead that individuals share in a cultural world; they communicate among themselves through the medium of their own group image (however conscious or unconscious it is). And, to a degree, they shape themselves in terms of this image because man makes himself through his own symbolic creations.

The point of our study is simply that people formulate their perceptions into what might be called an "experience," a life or a world, and that a radical new formulation seems to be taking place in our suburbs. The first part of this hypothesis, that people formulate their perceptions, is easily overlooked, precisely because it refers to something so intimately present that it has the hiddenness of the air we breathe. People form their experience—a pedestrian observation, yet ignored, especially by expansive Americans who are so busy forming experience that they become unaware of the fact of the process. And along with this unreflective activity among us, there is the naïve realism of our conventional understanding of man's experience. We tend to believe that experience is a datum impressed on the mind's photographic plates by out-there reality, when in truth experience is more of a fashioned thing, cooperatively created within individuals and groups as they encounter a mixture of "raw" realities. It is hard, for example, for suburbanites to comprehend that they are *making* the suburb; that is, that in their encounter with a novel economic, sociological, and ideological ("out there") situation, they are imagining and rationalizing a new ecological unit called "suburb," which represents a turning point in human history.

Suburban life is understandable; indeed, it exists for people only insomuch as they give it form. The work of this book has been to characterize some of the forms that are being given to this suburban life, thereby, hopefully, making these forms more self-conscious. Especially, we have been interested in giving self-consciousness and a certain degree of discursive, "objective" communicability to the ambivalent and playful form we call expansiveness.

In the soundings we flesh out this idea of expansiveness by looking at some of expansive man's artifacts: his politics, his aesthetic productions, his family life, his view of woman, his part in the university, his practical life, and his religion. We know, of course, that these artifacts do not come invested with little parables, little moral messages about the artist (expansive man). They are simply externally unconnected signals of his mentality. They are his diverse expressions in various areas of life. If he does have a "mentality," unrelated and independent as his artifacts are, they should suggest some minimal commonalities within his mentality, some functions that his style performs for him now and in the predictable future. In short, his artifacts should suggest his spirit and task.

Chapter 9

THE RADICAL CITIZEN

The Many Talents of Richard Nixon

President Nixon is a pubescent expansive man. He has many signs of being the first American President to exemplify suburban radicality. What his conscientious critics called the "demonsterization" of Tricky Dick during the strange (and tragic) campaign of 1968, we are inclined to call flexibility on his part, and a signal sample of America's new acceptance of a model of processional personality. Perhaps the high point of his demonstrable expansiveness during the first few months of his administration was his trip to Western Europe. Richard Nixon somehow amazed Europeans and Americans alike with his "new personality." While some journalists saw this new personality as a sign of hypocrisy, most, on both sides of the Atlantic, praised the American President for his adaptiveness. He had transcended his own (reliable) character. He was fashioning several new characters for himself, and his popularity in domestic polls went up accordingly.

He may or may not reach radical maturity, however. If he does not, his arrested maturation will cause him troubles of epochal proportions. There are some signs that suggest he is not on a steady course toward mature, guiltless expansiveness. For example, his address to the 1969 graduates at the Air Force Academy in Colorado Springs was fairly frightening. Out there under the crisp cowboy skies of Colorado, he delivered broadside attacks on the "new isolationists," a group that includes almost anyone critical of military spending. He was conscientious man appealing to the savagery of followers. Likewise, his huddles with the rigidly conservative directorship of the American Medical Association, his preachy statements on college disorders, his clearly ideological and rushed appointment of a new Chief Justice, and his principled drive for an antiballistic missile system on the eve of disarmament negotiations with the Russians: these may catch up with him as he brings us into the seventies.

To grow into and to maintain expansiveness can, in some situations, require plain old-fashioned courage. Expansive man does not form clear-cut, programmatic lobbies. Even when the politician somehow intuits that his constituency is largely expansive, conscientious organizations and savage tribes still come pounding at his door, and they can still promise disciplined support at election time. Radical styles for the politician, we believe, may "pay off," in fact, but their maintenance requires a kind of propless asceticism that is devoid of the colorful reassurances of conscientious saints and savage devils. The expansive politician must be prepared to suffer harsh personal attacks on his "integrity." He will offend both Arthur Schlesinger and William Buckley. They will regard his playfulness as vice and will tend to say so in highly moral encyclicals issued to their disciples. But the expansive politician can take heart: the day of ideological discipleship may well be almost over.

Our Quaint Village

Part of our national madness is interpreted by commentators under the rubric of "our cities are dying." Not having been able to usher in the age of reason in urban politics and economy, newsmen have decided to talk in plague language.

To a degree, expansive man helps create the dismal picture that the press is reacting to these days. Contrary to the hopes we expressed in the preceding section, expansive man is often not living up to his promise. Indeed, he at times can be perfectly regressive as he plays out his radical style. Take, for example, his pervasive nostalgia.

Harking back to simpler times, the radical suburbanite who is actively interested in political involvement is likely to secede from the metropolis, carve a village or township out of his part of the suburb, and then spend his energies as well as tax money supporting governmental divisiveness. The cities are in trouble now because the states have relinquished so little power to the cities. State legislatures have tended to encourage a plethora of local jurisdictions that remain, *in toto,* weak units in comparison to the state governments. And since the Federal Administration has apparently determined to promote "local control" by sending money through the governors and state legislatures rather than directly to the cities, the problem will be exacerbated. Metropolitan areas, in their infinity of divisions and overlappings—all with nearly zero power to tax—may easily become weaker and weaker.

In the face of the big city where he may gain his livelihood during the day, expansive man often tries to create little, town-hall government in the suburb where he sleeps, while magic words such as "participation" and "people power" serve to give a new touch to his basically nostalgic taste in politics. The disaster, of course, in all of this is that in the long run he is not at all protesting Big Government by his actions. He is helping Big Government (state and federal) to keep the relatively small governments in our cities in a prostitutional and moribund predicament.

Very likely it is expansive man (with all his votes and money) out in the suburbs that our dreary journalists really have in mind when they employ their frustrated and macabre rhetoric. Expansive man is opting out of the central struggle for people power in order to have time—when he is politically inclined—to make Hidden Hills the shiniest jewel of all the townships of twentieth-century America.

Freedom of Expression in the Suburb

It is true that the suburb is a repressive environment, because every human settlement, for its own joint survival, develops internal and external limitations to be imposed upon individual expression. Freud has made this truth into conventional wisdom. But when contemporary critics speak of suburbia's repressiveness, they mean that it is *unduly* repressive; it sets up unnecessary and inordinate limitations on expression. Our observations, however, make us uneasy with this generalization.

First, it is a valid point. There definitely are superfluous controls on expression in the suburb. However, one does not experience the sharpness of these controls in the relationship between the suburban whole and the individual. On the contrary, the kind of repressiveness that is being pointed to so much these days comes from the collision of various styles *within* the suburban whole, as, for example, when a savage principal tries to deal with expansive parents and students, or when a conscientious parent is laughed at by his expansive neighbors. Repression in the suburb is internecine, and therefore is superfluous, undue, and inordinate when it hits the individual. That is our first point—a repressed individual who describes his plight as being individually pitted against the entire suburb is simply inaccurate in his observations. Inevitably, he has neighbors who are allies. He is not isolated. It would be more accurate to describe him as engaged in a gang war.

Secondly, as a matter of fact the middle-class population of the suburb gives suffrage to a wider amount of expressiveness than is allowed anywhere else. The long-haired male who complains about the looks he gets from many of his neighbors should try living, say, in a peasant culture. Our romantic ideas about freedom-loving peasants to the contrary, the peasants would likely just kill him. Nowhere —in the city, on a farm, or on another continent—nowhere is there a greater range of allowable expression than in the suburb. (This goes also for criminal expression. Wayward children downtown, for example, are much more liable to a police "bust" than their suburban contemporaries.) The reason for suburban tolerance is the conscientious-expansive combine, an alliance that produces amazing permissiveness for individuals.

Conscientious man cannot do everything he might want to do to eccentrics. He is hamstrung by his commitment to "due process." Many legal authorities, teachers, and employers who want to retch at certain activities or certain physical fashions, nevertheless restrain themselves because of the demands of "due process." Expansive man, on the other hand, is likely to enjoy his eccentric neighbors; they are his comic kooks. He may even invite them to all his parties to add color. And he goes out of his way to have them in his sensitivity sessions so he can expand his relatedness. The conscientious-expansive combine leaves a lot of elbowroom for expression.

I Am a House

The radical suburb can tolerate, and even enjoy, topless bars, parking lots, freeways (or throughways), and shopping centers. But these must not be situated in such a way as to threaten the value of property. Likewise, radicals can tolerate extensions of civil rights—until property is involved. Then they join with their conscientious and savage neighbors to preach the gospel of sanctified soil. Suburbia presents an almost solid front on this issue.

For the artisan of morals, the house, the lot, and the backyard trees have a special importance. They are the immediate world that he has created, and the radical style is in the business of manufacturing environments. The expansive man is extremely aware of the changing, contrasting textures of his home, and his home is closely identified with his scale of values. He is, in fact, his home. Not just any house will do; he has given too much energy to forming the character of this one.

The struggle over property rights is a potential Waterloo for civic reformers, and they would be well advised to disassociate matters of property as much as possible from their projects. It would be well, for example, to separate quickly the financing of public education from the property tax. Otherwise, even expansive individuals will follow the expenditure of every penny with jaundiced eyes. Of course, property rights are tangential to almost any significant issue, and the middle class cannot forever ignore the abuses that are protected in the name of these rights. Still, we can expect the blood to flow whenever property is attacked explicitly. We had best be prepared, and had best look to our maverick sophists to help minimize the tensions.

Chapter 10

THE SUBURBAN ART MUSEUM

The War on Reason

A visit to almost any run-of-the-mill art museum will demonstrate that the world of art has traditionally been a quasi-military community. The walls are dutifully covered with the work of authorities (generals), and the work of lesser lights (privates) shows unmistakable evidence that they have marched to the orders of their superiors. The result has been an elitist, esoteric, rationalistic environment, where art objects have increasingly baffled the perception of outsiders, and where laymen believe themselves awkwardly unable to participate. They may feel artistic urges but are discouraged from even starting. They doubt both their understanding and their abilities.

By traditional lights, expansive man is aggressively antirational and anti-authoritarian. Usually his art appeals to the disproportionate; it spans styles and ages and encourages an environment of tactility rather than logicality.

The movement from pseudoclassical suburban art styles of a few years ago to today's array of environmental objects (statues, mobiles, metalwork, etc.) has to be described in martial terms: expansive man is engaged in a war on reason. Not long ago the suburbanite would have a few seascapes on his walls along with a stylized horse drawing, and on his end tables a neglected figurine, or mass-produced replicas from the days of Louis XIV. To have "real art" was too intimidating. Horse heads were always safe, but somewhere in school he got the idea that art is an esoteric and elite world into which only the aesthete may enter. The art world was viewed as something akin to pure research in mathematics. Now expansive man is challenging that idea. He is democratizing art ("everybody is doing it"), and filling his home with a variety of *functional* and environmental objects that simply feel good. He is working out his antirational intuitions by rejecting authority and consistency in art. He is willing to admit into his living room Picasso reproductions, junky tables, the horse head, his son's finger paintings, a Confederate dollar bill, and admire all of these together in an environment he calls artistic.

The day will soon come when expansive suburbanites will design their own interiors from beginning to end without any "expert" advice, whether hired or offered in the Sunday supplement. Art is taking a radically environmental turn; things fit into a texture of sensations, and there is no need to think that objects should have awesome credentials in order to be art. Many pieces of art are usable (silverware, rummage china, apple-crate furniture, colorful pillows); functional art is very much a part of the expansive household. All of this results in a dethroned position for professional art on the one hand and a massive inflation of artistic production and consumption on the other. But the producers are often not artistic in the traditional, professional sense. Art is expansive man's participatory democracy. If he is capable sometimes of tolerating repressive politics, he nonetheless believes in absolute egalitarianism and pluralism in the expression of feeling. Of course, the professional art world is making severe adjustments to this prolific but diversified market in expansive quarters. A new breed of artisan is emerging, a breed that produces touch-

ingly crude and unfinished work that in no way can take
on too singular a status in the expansive household environment. Expansive man tends to buy things that he
thinks he himself could make if he had time.

Instant traditions come and go. A kind of logical messi-
ness prevails. Expansive man buys his art objects in hard-
ware stores as often as he does in galleries. He might exhibit in his home a small collection of highly technical
op-art objects (that demonstrate scientific mastery of space
and perception) along with a purple toilet seat, a stuffed
owl, and a pinecone collection. Next week, he can sicken
of op art and purchase a three-dimensional, highly repre-
sentational grotesquerie of bats and coffins in its stead. By
past standards, he has no one taste in depth, and he is
slightly crazy.

If expansive character becomes the reigning ethos of the
1970's (and we believe it will), it will be lights-out for the
age of the superstar among artists. With the emergence of
expansiveness, moderately talented people will find a place
as artisans; fewer people will see art as a separate vocation requiring severe sacrifice. More will study art, enroll
in extension courses, take art as a college major or minor,
come together with friends to have "making" parties. Art
will be an absolutely necessary part of one's environment,
the area wherein expansiveness impresses its playfulness
on material objects. Everybody will be doing it. Art-making
will be as common as book-reading is today. We can expect, then, a general uplifting of the artistic factor in suburbia, but we cannot expect to be bowled over too often
by giants.

It Feels Good

As we entered the exhibition hall of the 1969 Design
West Show, sponsored by the California Museum of Sci-

ence and Industry, we were overcome with the desire to touch everything. Clearly, the makers of these objects were appealing to our skin as much as to our eyes. We knew intuitively that this was an invitation to lie and sit and roll and touch this environment. What an irony it was that the guards had deluged the place (even covering some art objects) with signs reading, WELCOME TO DESIGN WEST. . . . THESE OBJECTS ARE DISPLAYED FOR YOUR VISUAL ENJOYMENT. PLEASE DO NOT TOUCH.

Misunderstanding expansive man's pansensuality to be the highly specific and sexual sensuality of conscientiousness, the guards apparently thought that visitors would tear the place apart once they began touching things, even though most of the objects were quite monumental and unbreakable. That is how conscientious man overlooks the gentleness of expansive sensuality.

Two prim, middle-aged ladies, wearing long beads over their costly suits in a bid toward bridging the generation gap, stood gazing at a stool that the guards had corralled with a rope fence. The stool was covered with bear fur, and protruding out of the fur were about twenty baby-bottle nipples. The women could have been looking at a peaceful painting of the Grand Canyon. One sighed, "Oh, it's so sensual!" Before expansiveness, such a scene might have appeared to border on the pornographic. But expansive man is more innocent than that. He has unloosed sensuality from the exclusive grips of copulation. There are few leers in expansive art. The sexually pornographic in art will in the near future be the domain of a few conscientious intellectuals and their ill-educated victims. For expansive man, in the meantime, the necessary hierarchical distinctions for good pornography have been lost. He goes for calmer but continuous good feelings, and builds lush environments to provide them.

Grandma's Washboard

Have you noticed that suburban art seems to be celebrating the old-fashioned? More than one gallery owner has discovered lately that what really sells is not the *avant,* but the cornily realistic (American primitive) that our grandparents once had in their homes. A whole new small-business industry is springing up that distributes not antiques, exactly, and not junk, either, but something in between. Suburbanites are exhibiting their freshness and joy by filling their houses with dead people's tools, posters, and paintings.

It is almost as if the radical gains control over his murky past by surrounding himself with Grandma's mementos. He wants his wife on occasion to dress like Grandma. He regards as "arty" things that Grandma found toilsome: washboards, hand pumps, heavy, squeaky beds, and unbudgeable radio consoles. He plasters his kitchen with her crocheted prayers and primitive aphorisms. And, meanwhile, he often works in a streamlined, transistorized office building, planning weapons to annihilate the future. A most interesting interest in Grandma's world.

Chapter 11

FAMILY LIFE

The Peaceful Family

Expansive man is conservative when it comes to the traditional conjugal family structure. His radicality paradoxically bolsters the foundations of the conventional family unit, and he is thoroughgoingly old-fashioned in its defense.

Logically, one could argue that the opposite should be the case. More than others, expansive man is the son of science and pragmatism. Experimentalism has shaped his moral attitudes, and he does not tend to regard structures as God-given. Most strikingly, he seems to have a kind of casualness about the content of many traditional sexual mores. To him, for example, syphilis is a disease, not a naughty word or a spot on the soul; and he is often in the embarrassing situation of admitting to his children that he does not have a "reasonable" argument for this or that specific sexual-moral directive, and that he is not especially taken with the usual reasons presented for living the domestic life. Logically, his life-style and mentality, coupled with his disenchantment with traditional norms and taboos, should make him a marital nihilist.

But he is a conservative. He pours tremendous energies into his domestic life; strives to be a good spouse and parent; buys books that help him understand and promote familial relatedness; will go through psychotherapy and group counseling to learn to care better for his wife and children; and, increasingly, he is the grand arbiter and peacemaker. He does everything possible to fashion women's liberation, childish independence, and his own wandering interests into a peaceful alliance. He actually believes in and wants the proverbial "tranquil" family.

The reason for this, of course, is not religious or rational or mythical. The reason is pure accommodation. He often demonstrates an indiscriminate conservatism in the face of strife; he often seems to be a civil dropout because he is concerned not to let seriousness interfere with his play. For better or worse, family life provides the most effective personal basis for expansiveness in our society. It satisfies one's primal emotional needs, and thereby takes the wind out of potential savagery and even conscientiousness. It allows for a steady flow of ever-deepening personal relationships, rather than superficial encounters. It forces the suburbanite into contact with all age groups, especially the young. Most of all, it somehow provides a potentially secure springboard from which to leap into the world of diversity; it makes people feel safe, and then they can explore.

So it is to expansive man's interest to seek and to maintain a tranquil family life, which nowadays means that he must exercise a certain brilliance in accommodating his domesticity. Since he accepts independence for his wife, and independence for his children, his problems are cut out for him. He has to be the best husband and dad in town.

Rites of Passage

Every culture has to find ways of initiating its youth, of ensuring that society recognizes their new adult status, and of making certain that adult responsibilities are properly assumed. In other words, every culture has to have rites of passage to provide for its own renewal and renovation. Up to a certain age, the child is viewed as a precious object to be cherished, protected, and nourished. But then the child must die and the adult must be born.

In middle-class America, there is great confusion about the rites of passage. Generally speaking, the rites are not—as in primitive societies—associated with a particular age, such as puberty. Rather, they are associated with ceremonies, such as getting married and/or getting into one's career. A suburbanite breathes much easier after the marriage of a son or daughter. Gone are the nights of worrying about unwanted pregnancies and overly late hours, and gone are the fears that youth will fall under bad influences. Likewise, it is assumed that getting a job is the ritual act of joining the Establishment, the beginning of fiscal responsibility, and the end of youthful hell-raising.

But expansive children have planned and executed their own rites of passage, and unlike primitive forefathers, they have not even bothered to invite their parents. Suburban youth grow up very quickly, and they consider it much too burdensome to wait until after graduate school to share the delights of adult responsibility and freedom. Indeed, many are almost thirty (puberty twice over!) by the time they hang their shingle up or decide that the time has arrived to settle into a stable family life. For many, going away to college is the rite, although increasingly the initiation is associated with graduation from elementary or junior high school.

The disagreement about when the rites occur has usually erupted into arguments about sex and dating privileges, but during the past few years the focus has moved to matters of civil responsibility and institutional decision-making. At the heart of the student protest movement is the youthful assumption that students are locked into a quasi-colonial, childlike status, in spite of the fact that they, for most practical purposes, have become adults. They are not satisfied when dormitory visiting regulations are liberalized, because the patterns of authority are not thereby altered. Occupation of campus buildings and walkouts are forms of power available to the politically weak, and their use is a sign that students would often prefer to consider themselves politically weak adults rather than cherished possessions of families and states. The frustration of suburban parents with campus unrest is that they expect campus authorities, boards of education, and civic officials to act severely, as with unruly children, and they cannot conceive of students assuming adult roles in policy-making. Yet faculty and administrators, who know and respect the fact that the rites of passage have already occurred, tend to act as political men, moving to negotiate, attempting to accommodate. Their pattern is identical to that used by middle-class employers in dealing with unionization movements of the early twentieth century, where there was little confusion about the adult status of contenders for economic power. But suburbanites do not share this clarity with regard to their students; and in their failure they merely build up pressure, because their youth feel they can no longer abide the childhood role.

How Are You Going to Keep Them Off the Grass with Words?

We trust that many readers have had the disconcerting experience of trying to construct an argument intellectually convincing to a teen-ager that one should not experiment, even a first time, with smoking marijuana. It has become part of the American adult's biography to have attempted, often futilely, to use words that carry weight against the experience of marijuana.

The trouble with many youngsters today is that they are

not savages; they cannot be scared by words and images. This fact has important ethical and pedagogical consequences. A large number of adults carry around in their personalities more than one character style. Even when they have become predominantly expansive, for example, they can exhibit minor strains of savagery. The moral ban on marijuana is often a manifestation of such a strain—a savage association of terms (marijuana, dope, filth, insanity, profligacy). We are at a loss to fabricate any sophisticated arguments to match the moral-causative force of our savage imagery. Furthermore, except in dire emergencies, most of us are above employing the out-and-out savage pedagogy under which we were tutored. Neither myths nor syllogisms are of any avail here. And our customary fallback, the appeal to expansive experience, is downright retrogressive if one wants kids not to tamper with pot.

Marijuana has become an ethical symbol for so many problems in our society. As more and more individuals build their moral lives on experience, as the expansive ethos blossoms, how do we maintain savage a priori prohibitions or legalistic limitations to activity? Naturally, the problem takes on real irony within expansive environments, in certain families and on certain campuses. How do responsible parties avoid being justly accused of hypocrisy when, rather inconsistently, they forbid even cautious experimentation with some forms of experience?

It is not easy, and sometimes it is quite tragic these days, to try to keep kids off the grass with words.

A New Puritanism

Expansive man accepts and approves the idea of his grandparents that sexual expression and sexual relationships comprise an area of life that is highly charged with moral meaning. He remains squarely in a venerable tradition that sees sex as the chief symbol of man's fidelity to normative ideals. The beginning and end of what man ought to be and do is represented in his handling of sexuality.

Therefore, expansive man does not subscribe to the "new morality" as it is vulgarly understood, nor is he a "situation ethicist" as that role is usually understood. He is disciplined. He is not a libertine. We might even say that expansive man, in his acceptance of the moral character of sexuality, is a puritan, a new puritan, but a puritan nonetheless.

But expansive man's puritanism does not author rule books about the content of sexual activity. Expansive man, compared to his grandfather, is not so interested in the plumbing of sexuality, nor in precise rules for pairing off. His sins are not sins against nature. His sins are against personality. He is intensely moral about the modality or style of his sexuality, lest he injure his or his lover's personality. To a degree, the stylistic puritanism of expansive man is what the much-noted "sexual revolution" is.

The clash of content with stylistic puritanism is pyrotechnic to say the least. To be the mediator in such a clash is to participate in high-level psychodrama. A twenty-one-year-old student comes to you with her difficulty. She has broken off a romantic relationship with a young man because they found themselves to be catastrophically incompatible, and even a certain loathing had emerged between them. But now she has a most difficult problem with her parents. She has disclosed to them that while she and her friend thought they were in love, they had slept together twice. But once their "love" began to dissolve they could not justify making love; they discontinued all passionate physical gestures and eventually broke up. The story has infuriated her parents. "If only you had married and then divorced him, we could accept it; or if you had had a real affair, we could forgive you. But what is this 'relation' talk?

If there is respect, is anything O.K.?" Both the girl and her parents have lofty moral attitudes toward sex, and it is therefore nearly impossible to reconcile them. Puritan is pitted against puritan in this clash, and unless one or the other form of dogmatism provides the reigning norm, this will not be an atypical story. Journalists will continue to write about the sexual revolution.

What is this "relation" talk? It is the verbalization of stylistic puritanism, and it projects new horizons for man's feelings of guilt. Our young woman would have been overwhelmed by guiltiness, perhaps even to the point of needing medical attention, had she continued an impersonal or unloving sexual arrangement. Her mother, presumably, would have the same feelings in an illegal or love-only affair. In each case the term "puritan" seems fitting. The girl we would call a puritanical artist, expansively fashioning her actions to promote personal relatedness and bodily respectfulness. The mother we would call a puritanical lawyer, conscientiously maintaining activity within traditionally definable channels (clear-cut legality versus clear-cut lust).

The New Discipline

The moral ideals of a class of people can be detected by attention to the kinds of things parents worry about in their children's behavior. For example, conscientious Catholic parents in the traditionalist mold can go into states of seemingly total anxiety over the question of obedience. Obey the nuns; obey your father; obey the store manager—to the minutest degree. And do your obeying with a smile, a right attitude. One of us taught in a Catholic high school for three years and frequently felt inadequate in responding to the fears some parents expressed regarding their youngsters' disobedient ways. The feeling was one of being up against the primal symbols of an entire moral universe of terrible importance that was alien to us. Especially frustrating in these encounters was the experiential awareness that other parents of youngsters from the same school did not worry much about obedience. Some worried about looks and had an almost savage concern over physical accouterments. Others worried over something called happiness. They wanted their children to be happy, period. But perhaps the largest class of worriers were those who were anxious that their youngsters be adaptable. These were the expansive worriers.

Adaptability is the way suburban radicality often manifests its sense of discipline. It can be observed in parents whose anxious eye is on the lookout for any rigidity in their child's behavior: rigidity in food tastes, clothing, friendships, school interests. Rigidity in almost any form is considered problematic, an incipient psychological disturbance. The expansive parent is not worried so much about superficiality in his child's personality as he is worried about narrowness—any signals that the child cannot adapt quickly as new experiences are thrown to him.

Considerable time, money, and mental energy are consumed in developing adaptable children: new sleep schedules, new foods, new recreations, visits to a counselor. Like any effort to instill a discipline in youth, communicating the new discipline, adaptability, takes much energy out of parents. Adaptability, after all, if it is not to mean simply the loss of selfhood, requires considerable aesthetic savvy. Like an artist who is open to many media and many materials, yet is anxious to maintain his notion of himself as "this" artist, the adaptable person requires constant care.

Racism's Potential Contribution to Child-raising

The more or less pervasive leveling tendencies of public education (with some remarkable exceptions in affluent model units) run counter to the eclectic image of the good life. The eclectic image signals the downfall of the melting pot ideal or myth for America. The radical is a chronic pluralist, reveling in and testing the limits of variety. So it is no surprise that many suburban parents, taking the cue from their children, are talking about experimental schools. As long as problems of financing can be mentally bracketed out, one can always count on a fascinating evening of discussion by suggesting that suburban friends imagine the kind of school that they could invent and maintain.

Concurrently with suburban experimental-school talk, there is a more serious development arising in savage circles close to the legislative engines of our national destiny. There is, briefly, a drive to provide money to parents so that they can send children to a school of their own choosing: a racist plan, to be sure. But should this plan be realized, and should it be extensible to all areas of the land, it could have enormously positive consequences.

We mean that this plan, racist in origin, could be appropriated by an expansive-conscientious coalition of whites and blacks. Imagine, for example, the promise in a black parochial or private school system. The phenomenal success of the Catholic school after the nineteenth century in preparing minority peoples to wrestle with America while keeping their own identity could not be duplicated now in the private setting and under present economic circumstances. A private system is simply too expensive and tends to fall short of the public alternative. With public aid, however, there is little question that the parochial and private systems could become the laboratories in which even the wildest possibilities for educational renewal might be tested. These systems are fighting for their very survival and need to distinguish themselves experimentally. Public education is simply too saddled with bureaucratic lethargy, tax problems, and political pressures to test interesting, extremely different ways of doing things in the educational process.

Some of My Best Friends Are Sick

It is commonplace that psychic illnesses are aggravated in environments wherein the neurotic or psychotic is regarded as alien, bedeviled, fearsome. And it is no bold statement to say that such has been the predominant American environment. At least to the casual observer, public-supported mental health facilities seem to have often been designed and maintained to incarcerate witches. As a doctor who works at one of the nation's largest mental hospitals told us, "People come in here with problems. Then we make them sick."

Now and then newspapers will run a series of articles on this disgraceful situation, or a major network will do a one-hour special, and there will be a revival of reformism. Usually, though, nothing much gets done, because, as a people, we are not overly concerned about the seriously neurotic or psychotic person. We cannot even imagine him. Indeed, we are afraid of him. The directions of our education, our family training, and our religious upbringing have instilled in us the conscientious ethic of consistency. Eccentricity, in this ethic, is a failure; it is to be corrected by the imposition of rationality. The one who is not rational in an accepted sense gets a "D" or "F." And many of us have received, along with this rationalism, heavy doses of mythical fears about the emotionally eccentric. He is possessed. How many of us, for example, have had a close relative about whom we must not talk?

Sympathy has to do with the ability to imagine bizarre life-styles and alternative personalities for one's self. As young people are progressively liberated from the hierarchical model of personality, as well as from savagely instilled phobias concerning eccentricity, we can hope that they will convert their standard living environments—the suburb for example—into therapeutic centers wherein suffering and healthy imaginations can grow together.

The Well-cluttered Home

In preradical days, furnishing the home was the ritual act in which families declared their characters, and in which potential friends could find clues as to whether their families temperamentally might be compatible. Early American furnishings signaled the presence of warm bunny personalities committed to fireside camaraderie, to family togetherness, and to values rooted deep, deep in the friendly past. Modern furnishings, in contrast, were a bit zippy. They belonged to the young (in heart) crowd, and to families that had not been released from the need to flaunt their libertine ways.

One of us, in college, knew a young man who had carefully imagined the decorative design of his projected Shangri-la. It was to be Early American, and he had already spirited into his dormitory closet little Yankee, maudlin objects that would someday fit the scheme. His plan: to find a wife with similar tastes. What fun they could have refinishing their splintered butter churn and weaving their God-Bless-America rugs.

We visited him a few years ago in his brutally contemporary abode. Every surface was suited for dusting, and it was easy to see that here was a family very much in the Lysol generation. Like alumni returning to their rebuilt campuses, we knew that the old relationship was not the same. He was a different man.

For the Lysol generation, the premium in home furnishing was on consistency. If decoration was the expression of character, to be eclectic was to let all the world know about one's schizophrenia. Madness was not to be exalted, so homes slavishly followed a unifying theme. The world could tolerate a consistently nondescript home environment, complete with bread-and-butter, mediocre furniture. But, please: better people planned their homes to create a clear-cut mood.

In the 1950's, though, liberal suggestions were in the wind. "Don't be consistent in buying all your furnishings out of one period or one style." Consistency could be achieved in other ways: for example, using casualness, formality, or joyfulness as unifying moods. One was enjoined to buy Early American, contemporary, Oriental, and Mediterranean objects, but always at selected levels of formality. This was clearly a transition in the great American process of declaring social character, and the movement was expansive. Where would it all end?

Probably it will end, here in the 1970's, with the despairing groans of interior decorators who are threatened in tangible economic ways by the advent of suburban radicality. Magazines devoted to home improvement now proclaim the expansive gospel in every issue. They tell us to forget consistency, which is really a restrictive loyalty, and to make homes into monuments to our own diverse interests. People with good taste can be trusted. They can use a collection of objects and they can rest in their conviction that everything will somehow fit together. The fittingness is like that which characterizes the aesthetic unity of the radical personality—the unity of jangling but also surprisingly complementary styles.

The radical home is well cluttered. It is filled with objects people want to feel, articles found on the beach, as well as a number of other interesting, well-designed pieces.

Who cares if Grandma's rocker sits on a tiger-skin rug? And who cares whether matzo-ball soup is served in Arab cups? The radical cares, but not in the same way as did interior decorators in days gone by. Expansive man likes the combination, because it gives expression to his own life-style.

Chapter 12

WOMAN

What About Woman?

The arrival of suburban radicality could have been adequately studied solely under the rubric of "expansive womanhood." The conventional outlines of the so-called feminine role are drawn in conscientious and even savage strokes. As the expansive mentality becomes prevalent, the picture changes considerably. Woman's self-image as well as male attitudes toward her go through changes that are at least as revolutionary as, for example, the masculine relinquishment of the old idea of vocation.

In the first place, expansiveness completes the desacralization of woman, a process already begun in conscientious quarters. The extreme experimentalism of expansive mentality thoroughly integrates women into the real, playful world. The concept of mutuality and partnership is no longer an ideal; it becomes concrete, because it is a necessity. In fact, it is most often the women who introduce the men to expansiveness. In any case, a special impersonal and sacred place for woman is out of place, because she will not stand for it. She must be at liberty to test and experience all the possibilities affluence gives her. But her liberation is nonideological; it does not come on strong like a feminist movement. It is just there. She participates in the fun.

Expansive woman, in other words, is not expected to maintain the traditional role of fluctuating between the Virgin Mary and Eve. On occasion she tests her potentialities for entertaining male fantasies, but that gets boring as a full-time job. There are too many things to experience; too much to do, along with men; her role is not sacred; it is expansive. And expansiveness does not run along gender lines; it is personal.

Guiltless Womanhood

Expansiveness not only frees woman from the extremes of savage sexiness and savage exaltedness, each rooted in the male's murky projections of guilt, it also frees her from the recent more pervasive guiltiness of conscientious goal achievement. The dynamics of her new radicality cast out such male-oriented devils as stereotyped images of the hardened career woman. Why, more and more women are asking aloud, should I feel guilty about living experimentally? Why not dabble in education? Why not learn about nuclear physics? It is no secret that suburban wives are becoming more widely educated than their specialist husbands, as the wives dislodge themselves from conscientious-hierarchical thinking that demands narrowness and requires guilty reactions to experimentation.

The suburban woman is the primary beneficiary of the affluence and technical skills her husband labors to produce. Expansiveness allows and legitimates her exploitation of these benefits. Conscientious critics manage to stir up periodic waves of feminine guilt over the blessed state of womankind, but that is nonsense, the legacy of male jealousy and shortsightedness. A tremendous reservoir of playful female energy is being released in the suburbs. It has impressive possibilities, provided it keeps its self-confidence. For instance, it is altogether possible that women will reform the structures of our city governments and education systems. Where men, working out of liberal guilt, have failed, playful women may succeed.

Come Clean with Pornography

The poetry of liberation takes strange forms. Liberation has to do with changing the structure of perceptions, seeing with new eyes. Thus in a consistently patriarchal and aggressive Chinese society the authors of the celebrated *Tao te Ching* emphasized the values of femaleness, softness, and weakness for the king and wise man. The poetry of liberation throws one off guard and causes wonder. By doing violence to our common sense, it gives us respect in the Latin sense of the term, which means to look twice, to do a double take.

The volume of pornography that has recently found acceptance in suburban entertainment can be regarded as liberating. Once the whole demonic subject of woman-as-sex-object has been aired and sloshed about in all its explicitness, some of the greatest barriers to woman's personal relatedness to man are overcome. The hyperspecific sexuality of conscientiousness is toned down, and personal discussion can begin.

In his famous autobiography, Henry Miller made a most interesting transition between the volume entitled *Sexus* and the next volume, *Plexus*. The first volume rushes the reader through six hundred pages of the most explicit sexual description and erotic explosiveness in English literature, only to spill into the quiet, reflective tones of the second volume. It is as if Miller wants readers to get a few things straight and honest before he will really expose himself. He wrenches the snideness out of readers to prepare them to watch the deeper workings between men and women.

The new license in film and literature batters our perceptions of womanhood. When it is all said and done, when the implicit has been disrobed, there is nothing left but persons. The artist, of course, need not have such elevated intentions, but he has positive effects on woman's liberation whenever he outruns man's powers to sneer.

_____

Chapter 13

UNIVERSITY AS PROTOTYPE

Going to College to Prepare for College

A quick disturbing thought: the knowledge imparted to college students is already dated before it is imparted, and will have little or no connection with the knowledge students will need in order to function effectively and humanely in technological society one year after graduation. A second, less disturbing thought: students know it.

The fantastically ephemeral value of the information and even the wisdom of college years contributes to the emergence of suburban radicality. Young men and women are coming to know full well that they are in no wise being prepared for tomorrow, that they are not learning their vocation, and that the thing to do, even on the eve of graduation, is to be open to shifts from one irrelevant college major to another so as to keep the present interesting.

So, alas, the slowness of the higher education establishment in adapting itself to the present and predictable future is actually a boon for students. They are being prepared to live expansively without any illusions about permanence. Their apprenticeship could be easier and less cluttered, but hardly more effective. Because of its nonadaptiveness, the university may never again take on the charismatic and paternal aura it once had. Instead, it is a painfully faithful reflection of the real world, where institutions no longer provide suitable locales and models for nurturing an integral character.

Administrators as Good Guys

Fall, 1964, was the semester that students at Berkeley took on university president Clark Kerr and precipitated the election of Ronald Reagan, the demise of Kerr, the nationwide period of campus disorders, and the election of other Ronald Reagans to all kinds of public offices all over the country. (Meanwhile, Kerr and Mario Savio, his youthful protagonist, are off quietly doing their own things somewhere.)

Unfortunately, the original polarities of protracted battles often tend to guide our understandings for the duration. Many people, especially within our universities, still think that the contest is between Savio (a student) and Kerr (an administrator). Of course, such a perception of the problem is extremely consoling to faculty members, but it is also extremely misleading.

The battle has taken a new turn, and only the more perceptive students and a few administrators seem to be cognizant of this fact. The real war party is the faculty, because faculties are one of the last strongholds these days for unalloyed conscientiousness of style; and they are the surest to have to make uncomfortable adjustments should university reform take place. Consequently, it is typically faculties that obstruct change, in subtle and not-so-subtle ways.

Professors are usually baptized and confirmed conscientious men. They dedicate themselves to the spiritual life of hierarchical reason and to professional loyalty. They get paid to sit alone and write articles for the few. Their creed

is the liberal one, but in the face of expansive aliveness
(for example, the threat of student participation) or tribal
criticisms (as when local right-wingers question the curriculum's ideology), they become vehemently unliberal,
close ranks, subtly punish students, and issue bitter denun-
ciations to be votively disseminated by the liberal press.
And all the while they tell students that, if it were not for
the tense administrators, beholden to trustees, there would
be significant changes and a novel openness in the process
of higher education.

The search for truth, according to the conscientious way,
turns out to be quite sedentary. Thus, the trustiest way for
faculty types to obstruct reform is to sit. The furiously un-
responsive system that students find themselves resisting is
the product of overpowerful faculties who will not move,
in spite of what presidents and deans might believe to be
the imaginative, prudent course of accommodation.

We do not wish to overstate the case. Certainly there are
obstructionist students ("I am here to get an education")
as well as destructive administrators (often appointed by
vengeful politicians and stone-age regents). But in general, administrators tend to be expansive persons interested in change and compromise, while faculties struggle to
maintain an aristocracy modeled on the conscientious lad-
der of being.

Hard as it is to conceptualize (because most of us are
still rerunning the Savio-Kerr war films), administrators
are capable of creating a minority coalition along with students in the interest of reforming the teaching staff. After
all, administrators are customarily not brilliant scholars
who found satisfaction in the sacrificing life of research.
They are, rather, men who find their personal and mone-
tary satisfactions in solving problems, in getting along with
diverse characters, and in respecting experience. Their high
I.Q.'s are measured, not on the angelic scale, but on the
radical scale. And they are likely to be open to values from

the strangest of quarters. As one celibate Jesuit university president said, "You can trust the Black Student Union kids because they have a healthier sex life than the white students."

Hail to Thee, Our Alma Mater

If angry protesters would desist for just a moment, we would like to offer an appreciative word about American universities. At the risk of sounding mossback, we would even like to salute universities as pioneers of the present characterological revolution.

Academia knows what the middle class is doing, because it has lived for years with a similar style. Only when it annually celebrates the departure of jaded seniors does the university somehow manage to look like a coherent institution with a coherent set of traditions. For most of the year, the alma mater does its task in a manner reminiscent of war games. Departments are usually aware of other parts of the university only when there are battles to be fought; and assorted dogmatisms are always competing for control of curriculum-building and recruitment. Academia constitutes a menagerie of specializations and methodologies, all of which vie for the precious loyalty of students and grant givers. This is protean territory—with a vengeance.

Conscientious academics are always pushing interdisciplinary projects, because they have a difficult time living with the protean style. They wish that the university could at least operate with a harmony of interests, and could find places where disciplines might cooperate to everyone's advantage. Wisdom cannot be neatly divided along departmental lines, they say, and there surely is a need for bringing together the insights of specialists.

The trouble with interdisciplinary projects is that they

seldom work. Specialists quickly lose interest, or they become exasperated with the shoddy habits of those from other departmental tribes. When projects hold together beyond the first meeting, hours are consumed in translating the jargon of one field into that of another.

Interestingly, the most stable interdisciplinary activity proceeds when specialists never meet—that is, when students wander across an incongruous schedule of classes within different departments. Students are often frustrated in this trek and would like some conscientious soul to explain how the whole conglomeration fits together. But soon they learn to live with the absence of connectedness, and even find that the style guards them from prematurely dismissing valuable perspectives. Senior seminars that try to synthesize the students' motley experience are usually colossal failures, or at least, disturbingly superficial.

The chaos of undergraduate education is beautifully radical, and few are interested in making the university into a gigantic interdisciplinary project. If anything, there may be a need to man the radical barricades against the last bastion of conscientiousness in academia: graduate education. Why should universities encourage radical styles in undergraduates, then force them to repent? The barriers among departments are very high in graduate education, and departments feel threatened when "foreigners" are able to master inside skills.

Have we two educational ideals in competition here? Somehow, it seems strange that educators fail to see that their conscientious graduate programs are breeding methodological dogmatists—in a period when the most important discovery is perspectival multiplicity.

Alma mater has a problem, then. It must train specialists to maintain the eclectic academic game and to meet the demanding requirements of a technological society, yet it increasingly sees the need of multidisciplinary teachers who can see the larger picture. If the problem appears paradoxical, that is all right. Old Alma mater is learning to live with paradox too.

Let's Not Talk About Academic Freedom

Defenders of academic freedom can do more harm than good to the cause of liberty on university campuses. Whenever they raise the doctrine, they also inevitably initiate a discussion about academic responsibility and the limits of freedom—subjects that sometimes must painfully be raised, but that are best ignored.

There is always some indefensible academic practice going on at a university. For example, somewhere on campus there is bound to be a swashbuckling liberal who preaches his message daily, a philosophy professor who conducts therapy sessions, and a physicist who crusades against the doctrine of divine creation. Each, in his own way, is on the border of academic respectability, but each immeasurably enriches the experience of adolescents in their undergraduate trials. If one tries to become precise in delineating what is acceptable, too many interesting possibilities are ruled out.

A better strategy for champions of the cause is to keep quiet most of the time. When tempted to rise in righteous indignation, they should remain seated—glowering, perhaps, but silent.

The moments will come when silence should be broken. But the silence should be valued. It keeps the air cleared for pluralism.

White Is Wonderful?

The usual assumptions about American higher education have it that the university is a monument to white accomplishment and white awareness, and that black- and brown-awareness movements on campus are attempts to help minority students gain the kind of self-confidence and cultural pride that their white colleagues have instilled in them by merely attending the university.

The experimentalist-minded white student who wanders into a Black Studies course or attends a lunch-hour symposium on Mexican-American culture knows that the opposite is often the case. He knows that his upbringing and education have joined together to rob him of any specific cultural awareness, that they have denatured him and even taught him to feel guilty about his hollow whiteness. He learns very soon that participating in ethnic-studies experiences is not a visitation to a disaster area, nor is it a remedial sort of exercise for the backward. It is a celebration of richness.

There is a growing dis-ease with white guilt on the campus. Some schools have even witnessed the beginnings of what can be called "white studies programs," initiated by progressive students who are not acting out of chauvinistic intents, but are rather expressing a longing to taste and enjoy their cultural history. This development is fully in line with the dynamics of the new radicality. Nothing good, it is felt, can come from guilt. The basis and mainstay of playfulness is self-confidence.

Chapter 14

THE PRACTICAL LIFE

The Friendly Pathologist

Some jobs seem perfectly cut out to symbolize the radical suburb. One is medical pathology. First of all, there is the explosion of services that the pathologist must perform. At one suburban hospital, the pathologist started ten years ago with twelve assistants in his laboratory. At that time the hospital cared for about nine thousand patients a year. Now the hospital cares for ten thousand patients a year, an increase of only 10 percent, but there are forty-five assistants in the pathology laboratory. The reason: there are more things that the pathologist can do now, and potential technological services very quickly become needs, even rights. The medical pathologist has to keep up. He must constantly develop new skills, new tools, and imaginative ways to work within the same floor space he and his twelve assistants had a decade ago.

In addition, the medical pathologist is a businessman, scientist, librarian, teacher, and diplomat all rolled into a single packet. Obviously, he captains a small corporation and deals with an awesome collection of salesmen and tax collectors. But he must also be an expert. He is a scientist; he does much of his own research; he is expected to contribute to the collective knowledge of pathology. People who write textbooks in pathology are not often medical school professors; they are practicing pathologists. The pathologist is a librarian and a teacher. He must know quite a bit about every medical specialty employed in the life of the hospital. All the specialists and physicians come to him for information and advice about problems in their fields. Likewise, he must be the expansive diplomat par excellence, dealing directly with medical people and lay administrators, government and professional associations, employees, and other hospital departments.

His politics, moreover, cannot be too well defined. In order to function, he balances a multitude of other people's emotional fixations. He must live with the A.M.A. preflooders, while being himself the embodiment of coming socialized medicine. He must work fifty to sixty hours a week, because he loves his crazy business. And he must not manifest scorn toward surgeons, some of whom put in fifteen hours a week and complain about welfare loafers while sitting around drinking coffee in the pathologist's lab. The pathologist, in short, must be polymorphously flexible, not only in his professional knowledge (as he is pulled into the twilight zones of nuclear medicine), but also in the whole social world he builds around his laboratory. For him, expansiveness is as hammer and nails are to the carpenter.

Advertising, Art, and Ethics

Perhaps the professional artist of our time is the adman. He is hired by the modern Medicis to do high-quality and unusually independent work, but all for the honor and glory of the Medicis. His is an imagination for hire.

Because of its omnipresent influence on our attitudes and decisions, advertising, almost everybody recognizes, has a crucial ethical importance for us. And since advertising is so closely aligned with art, its ethical importance is compounded. Art touches us on the intuitive level; it gives shape to our feelings. It is, from an intellectualist viewpoint, pre-ethical, yet it invades moral motives and acts. This is no new doctrine. In the nineteenth century, Nietzsche reminded people that ethics and aesthetics are one.

What is new is the pervasive effectiveness of modern advertising that exploits the powers of art. Admen are our chief ethicists. They both describe and prescribe our moral living, and they do so through the forms of intuition.

In listening to expansive persons report the process of personal decision-making, we are struck by the aesthetic terminology employed. Our impression is that expansive man imagines himself as his own adman, selling himself to himself as a beautiful artifact. Whether he is simply self-deluded may be one of the central issues of the final years of the twentieth century. Freedom for expansive man consists in the ability to write his own ads independently of the professional. His success is as yet undetermined.

Thou Shalt Be Mobile

The ever-extending frontiers of the suburb could make an interesting study in aerial photography. An accelerated-time film would show the suburbs spreading like jelly across the land. Tract after tract is developed. Mobility is a key component of the suburbscape and the greatest threat to suburban economy is the slowdown of suburb spread. Nothing throws people into panic more quickly than does the threat that building loans will be curtailed.

It is fitting, then, that the advertising industry appeals to the sense of mobility. Products are pushed for their capacities to help you get away, move, swing with the swingers. Indeed, an evening of TV commercial-watching or a glance through news magazines could lead one to the conclusion that if expansive man has traces of savagery and mythical thinking, they certainly are manifested in his craze for mobility.

Advertising both utilizes and confirms the expansive eleventh commandment: thou shalt be mobile. But, what about old people? Try watching the commercials with old people in mind. The pathological potentialities become immediately apparent. Expansiveness does not prepare people to age, and it does not prepare the young to live with the aged. Sick as it might sound, our observation is that expansive man too often ironically combines his nostalgia with a disregard for and even repugnance at old people.

Nobody Wants to March in Line Anymore

Armies, police forces, and other quasi-military institutions are organizations run by conscientious men (officers) who use expansive rhetoric to obtain followers, who in turn are expected to have savage loyalties. That is to say, armies and police forces are in trouble.

Traditionally these institutions have operated smoothly on a mixture of savage and conscientious styles. That will not do anymore. Expansive man is muddying the picture, and the institutions have not yet adapted to his presence except in the most superficial of ways: recruitment literature sounds expansive.

"You'll probably have a busier social life than ever before. . . . You can get together for dancing, a songfest, cards, bowling, golf, tennis, you name it—on any Army post!" If you are a WAC, your wardrobe will be designed by Mainbocher. And as a Marine, "Paris is only one of many overseas posts where you could be stationed." "Some young men are happy just to kill time, but not an 'action guy'; he makes things happen by joining the Action Army."

(Hopefully he will not be happy just killing *people*.) And supposing Paris, Spain, or French Morocco sound boring; try the Navy instead of the Marines. "Blast shields, vibrating flight decks," "jets scream down the length of the cat" —aircraft-carrier duty is "exciting." According to the Jack Webb TV commercials, if you become a Los Angeles City policeman, you will be doing things on your free time like flying in a glider, scuba diving with your beautiful wife, and looking extremely intelligent and virile. You will be a kind of Teddy Sorensen–John Wayne.

The whole drift of our youth-nurturing practices does not prepare youngsters for long-term savagery. The church, for one example, in its parish life, was once a very effective training ground for future policemen and soldiers. Nowadays an effective high school religion program is as likely to turn out expansive passive resisters, and a few full-blown conscientious objectors.

Of course, police forces are in more trouble than armies. The latter still have the draft, terror, and military prisons. Nobody has to be a policeman. As police groups isolate themselves more and more from "outsiders," the people whom they are pledged to serve, the situation worsens. As long as they play Tribe, only potential savages will want to join, Jack Webb notwithstanding.

Adolescent Engineers

The suburban radical extends the experimentalism of adolescence into his adult life, because he has been economically freed to dedicate a considerable portion of his time to play. An extreme example of this adolescence can be observed in the growing suburban class of engineers who actually are paid, and paid well, to play at work. These are the children of federal contracts. They are provided with billion-dollar allowances to find interesting problems and pursue them. They constitute a veritable teen club funded by remarkably indulgent parents. It is amazing to listen to engineers talking about their work—technical problems are to them as Coke and chocolate are to a fourteen-year-old, minus skin eruptions. And there is always father to provide money and transportation to the candy counter.

One major company we know consciously attempts to keep its engineering talent in a recreational mood. Thousands of its employees, of course, are fascinated with their microproblems within the huge process of building missiles to carry atomic bombs. The more playful and experimental these individuals are, the more secure the contract's renewal. But for those engineers who have qualms about designing weapons during recreation time (interestingly, several engineers in this group are ex-military officers), the company has other contracts. A man might express disillusionment over the potential destructiveness of his work, and he will soon be given a job working on anti-forest-fire systems, or on a state-contracted analysis of public welfare, or on a harbor-improvement study.

There is, from a conscientious perspective, a widespread irresponsibility in the engineering profession. Paternalistic government sets down the wide parameters of engineering games, and then all involved jump in wholeheartedly without any answerability as to the overall intents of the game. As might be expected, nobody has come up with very practical alternatives to this irresponsibility, and it does appear to be, for the most part, irreversible.

What we can *hope* for, though, is that Father, the Government, might decide to set loose this fantastic reserve of adolescent playfulness on problems like pollution, hunger, transportation, and international communication. If our expansive technocrats ever aim their playfulness at these problems, and are provided a livelihood for having this fun, it will be a new beginning for man: more significant than Neil Armstrong's footstep on the moon.

Cos Cob and Cerritos, U.S.A.

Cos Cob, Connecticut, does not have to brag about its wealth, about the power that its citizens wield, or about the fact that many of its residents are descendants of *Mayflower* stock. Everybody knows it. When you drive up the casual, forested lanes that lead off the Merritt Parkway, you are aware that this is an area carefully set apart. You cannot pop into Cos Cob—a hop, skip, and jump from the urban commonplace to this suburban somethingplace. The lanes take you past a pond and then steeply up a hill. It takes effort to get there.

Cerritos, in Southern California, is an expansive city, redesigned in the era of suburban radicality to suit the temperament of the new middle class. It used to be called Dairy Valley, because for years it served as a center for Southern California's dairy industry. But the name was changed, presumably to discourage memories of the terrible barnyard odors that used to emanate from there. Now the tract developers are in control. And suburb watchers have an unparalleled opportunity to witness what kind of design fits the current characterological temper.

Cerritos is no Cos Cob, but it has homes that rival Cos Cob's quality, and it has tracts that bring the beautiful and the rich into residential togetherness. The startling happening in Cerritos is that expensive tracts exist side by side with inexpensive ones, and it is not uncommon to find a lumberyard or junk shop immediately adjacent to a walled enclave of affluence.

In part, the reason for Cerritos' quiltlike design is that the lumberyards and junk shops were there first, the tracts being built on reclaimed dairy lands. (Think of the roses that will grow in *that* soil!) But this explanation is not sufficient. People, to our amazement, continue to buy houses that are so situated, and perpetuate the randomness of

Cerritos' strategy in locating tracts.

What Cerritos offers is a caricature of Cos Cob's self-enclosed conscientiousness. It cuts affluence off from association with particular geographical areas and discourages the development of a historical class-consciousness, bound to the past of *this* place.

Cerritos is nostalgic about the Cos Cob style. The builders have not given up the idea that rich people should live together, and that poor people have more in common with poor neighbors. But Cerritos laughingly plays with the nostalgia. It builds Cos Cobs, yet puts them next to lumberyards, and sprinkles in a few middle- and lower-income tracts for good measure. It enjoys the past by building old California-Spanish haciendas, yet refuses to establish a territorial basis for encouraging an awareness of class history tied to the hallowed acres of Hacienda Park Estates. Cerritos is radical. Its ecology is eclectic, and the personality that Cerritos is assuming cannot be interpreted in any other way.

One can imagine that future suburban renewal experts will gasp at their discovery that Cos Cob, Connecticut, has no junkyards to accent its stately mansions. How old-fashioned! Arise, Cerritos, and show Cos Cob what it is like to be thoroughly mod.

Chapter 15

FAITHS OF OUR FATHERS

A Modest Proposal for Protestants

Tucked away—far, far from the worshiping crowds at the local Protestant church—is a classroom we hardly dare mention. More often than not, leadership there is provided by hired personnel, mothers who would feel insecure elsewhere, fathers whose masculinity is slightly threatened by the environment, and occasionally by genuinely heroic teachers. This, alas, is the nursery. For a number of years, Protestant denominations have published excellent materials designed to transform nursery classes into occasions for imaginative learning. And in many cities and towns, churches have established weekday nurseries to develop experimental programs in preschool education. But the myth persists: educationally, this is the bottom of the heap—important, but mainly as a foundation for later lessons in the faith.

In contrast, teaching the adult class is a Major Accomplishment reserved for saints, imported speakers (whose unsavory characters are known only in home territories), ministers, retired generals, and learned gentlemen. Churches ministering to university communities hardly dare offer the post of speaker to anyone who has not achieved the rank of associate professor or at least a decent salary in a reputable business. Gone are the play centers, where you can fiddle away a few minutes with blocks, or where you can dress up in a white coat and try your hand at being a milkman without losing face. At the adult class, one endures hours of straight verbalization designed to provide a mature grasp of issues that were defined in an earlier, less expansive theological era. There, in that room with the hardback chairs, affluent radicals learn how to feel guilty about their radicality.

Expansive man would rather be in the nursery, or at least he thinks that Protestantism has a great deal to learn from its experience in preschool education. The preschool is literally the only place where Protestantism has systematically encouraged playfulness and found a theological dignity for the activity. And it is the only place where sensuality has not been utilized consciously as a means toward more spiritual ends—for example, creating an architectural atmosphere conducive to worship. In the nursery, children let sand drip through their fingers, draw with large crayons, and sometimes clap their hands. Why? Because the activities have much to do with the gospel; because that is what preschool children enjoy doing when surrounded by warm, accepting relationships within the community of faith.

In other words, Protestant nurseries tend to be expansive, and they are the prototype for directions that must inevitably be considered by Christian education establishments. *Avant* educators ought to be examining nursery curricula for signs of things to come, and more important, for theological insights long cherished by the mother church but not shared with the older sons and daughters, who only now are discovering the beauty of the body and of play.

Our modest proposal is that Protestant churches ought to inaugurate regularly scheduled, mass pilgrimages to their neglected nurseries. The treks should not be directed toward saving preschool education or toward recruiting needed nursery teachers. Instead, they ought to be shaped as occasions within which Protestant adults begin to consider new possibilities for their own growth, possibilities that do not entail the loss of toddler expansiveness. The nursery can no longer be considered the bottom of the heap. It has something of a mission to fulfill in providing models for conscientious but unimaginative ecclesiastical educators.

One, Holy, Expansive, and Apostolic

Among the Christian options, the Catholic Church is amazingly expansive. She is a giant of a woman: loving variety, unprincipled, pluralistic, proudly nostalgic, flaunting her inconsistencies, experienced, sensual, comfortable in any surroundings, and—most of all—she is endowed with the kind of healthy self-confidence that the expansive style needs.

In this book, we are discussing a tendency in life-style that we see as the regnant pattern for the future. But, throughout, we have tried to make it clear that this tendency which we call expansiveness largely has not yet elicited legitimation, whereas the competing tendencies in conscientious style and savage style have venerable sources of legitimation and self-confirmation. Interestingly, the Catholic community might be viewed as one area where expansiveness has powerful roots, wholesome self-awareness, and legitimation. Standard opinion would have people believing just the opposite: that Catholicism is predominantly conscientious or even savage in the collective and individual styles it spawns.

Even though this opinion often comes from Catholic circles, it is off base. Because of the general self-confidence of the Catholic mentality, Catholics can be quite ruthless when they are conscientious or savage, it is true, but the characteristic thrust of Catholicism is toward nonguilty expansiveness.

The Catholic community is low on content and high on style. Under a common (though rich and varied) liturgical umbrella, a whole zoo of ideologies and temporary commitments as well as contradictory moral norms are either blessed or compassionately ignored by the disagreeing. Conflicts are fought out in attempts to grab the podium, not by "honest" secessions; and except in some of the stagnant backwaters of Catholic scholastic rhetoric, rational consistency has never been an overriding concern for the Catholic mentality. The point has simply been to be a member of this supportive community; and one is a member, basically, merely by calling oneself a Catholic.

Instead of using principle to separate angelic man from creation, Catholicism offers pervasive rationalization of all life and of all styles of living. Behind an ordered worship and preaching, there is an almost mystical confidence in the chaotic universe: Just break bread together and then go, separately, and do your own thing.

Catholicism is glutted with symbols of nostalgic cohesiveness, and this fact makes it hard for many to see and appreciate the healthy playfulness generated within Catholicism. Eugene McCarthy and Generalissimo Franco, Robert Kennedy and Joseph McCarthy—each has practiced what he regarded as Catholic politics. Even Catholic theology, as done in universities, rather resembles something like a subdivision of the liberal arts with all their profuseness and fuzzy edges. Critics have simply overestimated the specificity of Catholic thought, and have underestimated the general matrix of independence that membership offers. That is, critics have paid too much attention to a minority of a minority (priests and bishops who take their uniformly bad education too seriously, along with a handful of Barthianized ex-seminarians) and have neglected to see how little *that* line (the combine of conscientious-conservative and conscientious-progressive priests, almost priests, and journalists) represents Catholicism's main direction, which is expansive.

Our hope, then, is that Catholicism will exploit its native strengths. Let it pour on mystery and nostalgia and compassion, keep finding ways of sensually ritualizing and blessing and rationalizing the pluralism of mentalities, and thus remain pregnantly suggestive of expansive models for all of us, as well as taking an integrative and balancing role for society during its transition period into greater expansiveness.

Disorganized Protestants and Creative Ministries

Present proposals to bring about church union among Protestant bodies have much merit. A certain straightening out of jurisdictions and the cessation of reduplicated services might bring many benefits and might even provide a stable future for the institutional church.

However, some of the present chaos leaves constructive openings for the mission of the church, and does allow for the kind of diversity that expansive man enjoys and will support. We have in mind an old downtown Methodist church that is now owned by a combined Methodist and Presbyterian group of parishioners, many of whom are from the suburbs. Because of the confusing ecclesiastical and liturgical jurisdictions, because of its proximity to a university and a black ghetto, and because of the support it receives from its commuting suburban faithful, this parish has developed a highly experimental worship life that combines the best of traditional and ethnic expressions with the heaviest and most revolutionary celebrations in town. Amazingly, the young and the old, the black and the white, are brought together in mutual awe.

This church is the result of organizational sloppiness. In

any regional perspective, it should be liquidated. But in the meantime, it is a manifestation of authentic Protestant religion: it civilizes people. And it does this because some expansive persons have taken it upon themselves to transform a shabby situation into a human celebration.

Paradox

In the second half of the 1960's, there was a popular but short-lived flurry of excitement over something called "secular theology." Secular theology repristinated a set of old phrases and attitudes about man having grown up. That is, secular man, compared to his predecessor, "religious man," is an adult; secular man does not believe that the universe is a big bowl; secular man is not afraid of ghosts; secular man is self-reliant (does not need a God); secular man is a realistic politician; secular man is not afraid of bishops; and secular man probably will do something about starvation, overpopulation, racism, atom bombs, the learning process, urban ills, cancer, and psycho-impotence. Naturally, upon hearing about secular man most of us became initiated secularists, with a whole new grown-up vocabulary.

What embarrassing memories! One of us remembers announcing the arrival of secular man to a high school religion class populated by intelligent suburban youngsters. Somehow secular man seemed a little uptight to them. "What's wrong with ghosts?" "Is he some kind of a machine?" "Didn't Nietzsche say that a long time ago when he was on a high or something?" "I'd rather keep up with Jesus and incense." These were brainy, modern young people. They already knew more about technological progress, for example, than most adults, and were fully prepared to use it and enjoy it. And contrary to so many theologians who are country boys, these young people grew up in the metropolis; they did not discover big buildings in graduate school or during an urban ministry. In principle, these youngsters are secular men; and they are in fact. But as it then turns out, secular man is profoundly religious. He is open to many forms of prayer. He is acutely aware of his dependence upon forces larger than himself, and he usually will not blush when referring to them as God.

It was more than a little bit embarrassing to find out that youngsters who would soon be off to places like Cal Tech, Stanford, and Berkeley were unhesitatingly religious. It was all the more impressive to see them return on vacation from these institutions with a deepened religiosity. In some cases, this regressiveness had even spread to parents.

This experience was especially interesting in the light of the fact that one of the chief axioms of secular theology was that a metaphysically oriented theology tends to be irrelevant to the present. We began to agree. But the puzzlement remained. We were sure that secular theology had spoken reliably for a few moments and for some people. But what, we asked, was happening now? Secular man was becoming something of a fervently religious soul. How could he, or we, justify this credulity?

The answer is *paradox,* an event or concept that runs counter to common sense, yet is somehow true. The people we were encountering were open to paradox. Such an openness, of course, requires both humor and detachment —and our friends and students had both because they were mainly expansive characters: first-line suburban radicals who had a general cosmic and religious piety that would shame a church mouse. Their apologetics, when they were forced into reflectiveness by our probings, were the apologetics of paradox. If you could believe in rockets, they would say, you could believe in the supernatural. If you could imagine blowing up the world, you could imagine a friendly world. If you could enjoy seeing *2001: A Space Odyssey,* you could enjoy going to Mass or meditating on the *Tao te Ching.* If you could talk about the United Nations or urban renewal, you could have I–Thou relationships with just about everybody. Why not? Your whole life is paradoxical anyway. Why become selectively reasonable?

Good Static

More than one critic has pointed out that what Catholicism needs is a good rationale for change, a theory that can justify transition. Such problems as contraception, they argue, are not so much matters of a debate over natural law as they are bafflements over the validity of any important change.

While there is great truth to this criticism, another point needs mentioning. Catholic individuals bring a great experimentalism to their piety, but there is also a static element in their faith and in their church that they find positively attractive. In some cases, this selective conservatism is the result of nostalgia. In other cases, it can be more serious: an expression of immortality, a way of finding continuity with life. Whatever the cause, Catholics have no adequate rationale for this static dimension of their experience. They are embarrassed at their own intuitions.

Among other things, Catholicism is in great need of a theology of permanence, a reflective legitimation of its most beautiful resources. Presently the Catholic theological field is populated by brilliant men correctly legitimating the process of change, and not-so-brilliant reactionaries. The result: Catholic progressives find themselves in the sad state of most white revolutionaries. They have little to bind themselves together except a common hatred of their past.

NOTES

1. Erik H. Erikson, *Identity: Youth and Crisis* (W. W. Norton & Company, Inc., 1968). Robert Jay Lifton, "Protean Man," in R. Cutler (ed.), *The Religious Situation: 1969* (Beacon Press, Inc., 1969), pp. 812–828.

2. Seymour Lipset, "A Changing American Character," in Michael McGiffert (ed.), *The Character of Americans* (The Dorsey Press, Inc., 1964), pp. 302–330.

3. See, for example, David M. Potter, "The Quest for National Character," in John Higham (ed.), *The Reconstruction of American History* (Harper & Row, Publishers, Inc., 1962).

4. William H. Whyte, Jr., *The Organization Man* (Simon and Schuster, Inc., 1956), pp. 365–381.

5. Philip Rieff, *Freud: The Mind of the Moralist* (Doubleday & Company, Inc., 1961), pp. 391–392.

6. See Philip Rieff, *The Triumph of the Therapeutic: Uses of Faith After Freud* (Harper & Row, Publishers, Inc., 1968).

7. Lifton, "Protean Man," *loc. cit.*, p. 812.

8. *Ibid.*, p. 816

9. See Th. Shcherbatskoï (Fedor Ippolitovich), *The Central Conception of Buddhism and the Meaning of the Word Dharma* (Calcutta: Susil Gupta, Ltd., 1961), pp. 21–22.

10. *Time,* June 13, 1969, p. 77.

11. Herbert Marcuse, *An Essay on Liberation* (Beacon Press, Inc., 1969), p. 26.

12. *Ibid.,* p. 38.

13. Norman O. Brown, *Life Against Death* (Vintage Books, Inc., 1959), p. 308.

14. *Ibid.,* p. 310.

15. Kenneth Keniston, "Social Change and Youth in America," in Erik H. Erikson (ed.), *The Challenge of Youth* (Doubleday & Company, Inc., 1965), pp. 201–203.

16. Ruth Benedict, "Continuities and Discontinuities in Cultural Conditioning," in Patrick Mullahy (ed.), *A Study of Interpersonal Relations* (Grove Press, Inc., 1949).

17. Erik H. Erikson, *Childhood and Society* (W. W. Norton & Company, Inc., 1964).

18. See particularly Herbert Marcuse, *One-Dimensional Man* (Beacon Press, Inc., 1964), Chs. 1–4.

19. Harvey Cox, *The Secular City* (The Macmillan Company, 1965), Ch. 2.

20. Ernst Cassirer, *The Myth of the State* (Yale University Press, 1946), p. 43.

21. *Ibid.,* p. 41.

22. Bronislaw Malinowski, *The Foundations of Faith and Morals* (London: Oxford University Press, 1936), p. 32.

23. Joe Flaherty, "The Ups and Downs of Jerry Quarry," *West Magazine,* June 15, 1969, p. 15.

24. *Ibid.*

25. Cox, *op. cit.,* Part Two.

26. Robert Jay Lifton, *Revolutionary Immortality* (Random House, Inc., 1968), Chs. 2–4.

27. Ernst Cassirer, *The Philosophy of Symbolic Forms: Volume Two: Mythical Thought* (Yale University Press, 1955), pp. 155–174.

28. *Ibid.,* pp. 235–261.

29. See especially Marcuse, *One-Dimensional Man,* Ch. 2.

30. *Ibid.,* Ch. 8.

31. *Ibid.*

32. Rieff, *The Triumph of the Therapeutic,* p. 242.

33. *Ibid.,* p. 241.

34. *Ibid.,* p. 232 ff.

35. *Ibid.,* p. 238.

36. *Ibid.,* p. 239.

37. H. Richard Niebuhr, *The Responsible Self* (Harper & Row, Publishers, Inc., 1963).

38. *Ibid.,* pp. 48–52.

39. *Ibid.,* pp. 52–54.

40. *Ibid.,* particularly Ch. 4.

41. See Ernst Cassirer, *The Logic of the Humanities* (Yale University Press, 1961), pp. 137–140.